JOSEPH CONRAD'S BIBLE

Joseph Conrad in 1896

JOSEPH CONRAD'S BIBLE

BY DWIGHT H. PURDY

UNIVERSITY OF OKLAHOMA PRESS : NORMAN

Publication of this work has been made possible in part by a grant from the Andrew W. Mellon Foundation.

Library of Congress Cataloging in Publication Data

Purdy, Dwight H. (Dwight Hilliard), 1941–
  Joseph Conrad's Bible.

    Bibliography: p. 151.
    Includes index.
    1. Conrad, Joseph, 1857–1924—Religion and ethics. 2. Bible in literature. I. Title.
PR6005.04Z7857   1984   823′.912   83-40331
ISBN 0-8061-1876-8

The paper in this book meets the guidelines for permanence and durability of the Committee on Production Guidelines for Book Longevity of the Council on Library Resources, Inc.

CONTENTS

For Jibby

PREFACE

Muriel Bradbrook's honed phrase, "Poland's English genius," gets to the heart of a matter. Probably through conscientious study, Joseph Conrad absorbed a culture and remade it in his own image. His art is an act of critical intelligence, a commentary upon all that is of the essence in English literary tradition. We study those essences when we study Conrad. This book considers one essence always acknowledged but seldom discussed, the rhetoric of biblical allusion. Revising the Authorized (King James) Version in his art, Conrad comments upon its vital role in English literature.

Quotations from Conrad's works are from the Dent Collected Edition. Quotations from the unfinished novel *The Sisters* are from the Crosby-Gaige edition, published in 1928. Quotations from the Authorized Version are from *The Interpreter's Bible.* Portions of this study appeared in different form in *Philological Quarterly, Texas Studies in Literature and Language, Conradiana,* and *Journal of Modern Literature,* copyright Temple University. I thank the A. S. W. Rosenbach Foundation, Philadelphia, for allowing me to examine the manuscript of *Nostromo* and the Humanities Research Center of the University of Texas at Austin for permitting me to quote from the manuscript of *Victory*.

This book is far the better for the detailed criticisms of Arthur Henry King, of Brigham Young University, and Laird Barber, of the University of Minnesota, Morris. I am also indebted to Alan W. Friedman, of the University of Texas at Austin; Leon Higdon, of Texas Tech University; and Avrom Fleishman, of Johns Hopkins University, for their reactions to earlier drafts of portions of this book. I have made my reader in their image—assuming a reader familiar with the Bible and intimate with Conrad.

Grants from the Graduate School of the University of Minnesota and from Elizabeth S. Blake, Academic Dean in the University of Minnesota, Morris, eased my labors, as did a single-quarter leave from the University of Minnesota.

It is a pleasure to acknowledge the good work of the Library Staff of the University of Minnesota, Morris, especially Barbara McGinnis, and of my typist, Kathy Cooper.

But I take greatest pleasure in acknowledging the debt of love expressed in my dedication.

Dwight H. Purdy

Morris, Minnesota

JOSEPH CONRAD'S BIBLE

Falstaff. Thou hast the most unsavory similes, and art indeed the most comparative, rascalliest, sweet young prince. But, Hal, I prithee trouble me no more with vanity. I would to god thou and I knew where a commodity of good names were to be bought. An old Lord of the council rated me the other day in the street about you, sir, but I marked him not; and yet he talked very wisely, but I regarded him not; and yet he talked wisely, and in the street, too.

Prince. Thou didst well, for wisdom cries out in the streets, and no man regards it.

Falstaff. O, thou hast damnable iteration, and art indeed able to corrupt a saint.

—William Shakespeare, *Henry IV,* 1.2.74-86

But the day of the Lord will come as a thief in the night; in the which the heavens shall pass away with a great noise, and the elements shall melt with fervent heat, the earth also and the works that are therein shall be burned up.

—2 Peter 3:10

"It began by me coming to you at night—like a thief in the night. Where the devil did I hear that?"

—Lingard, in Joseph Conrad, *The Rescue,* p. 398

INTRODUCTION

Joseph Conrad wrote for readers gifted, like Falstaff, with a fine ear for damnable iterations. His readers, or many of them, could answer Lingard's question (see also 1 Thess. 5:2; Rev. 3:3, 16:15) and laugh at his naïve blasphemy. His iteration defines "that man of infinite illusions" (*The Rescue*, p. 466). It also prefigures the parody of apocalypse that attends the dynamiting of the *Emma* and Lingard's romantic fantasies. When the *Emma* goes, we are supposed to hear Peter's verse again and the opening of the sixth seal (Rev. 6:12): "The heavens split over [d'Alcacer's] head with a crash in the lick of red flame; and a sudden dreadful gloom fell all around the stunned d'Alcacer, who beheld with terror the morning sun, robbed of its rays, grow dull and brown through the sombre murk which had taken possession of the universe" (p. 442). Thereupon the feckless Belarab mounts "a fiery pony" and dashes forth in "triumphal progress" (p. 443)—Christ of the white horse, his eyes "as a flame of fire" descending from heaven to a new earth (Rev. 19:11-15). Finally, Lingard imagines that his brig has been touched by "the very wing of the Angel of Desolation"

(p. 453), the angel of the seventh seal (Rev. 16:17) sent to announce the coming of the thief. Conrad's iterations describe a circle about Lingard's illusions.

The Rescue, and much else in Conrad, requires a Falstaff's ear. Very few readers have it today. Theodore Ziolkowski, in his excellent *Fictional Transfigurations of Jesus,* regrets the loss:

But it is the rare individual under fifty who can claim to be *bibelfest* in the sense of earlier generations. It is characteristic that our schools today, while they often teach classical mythology or the ceremonial rites of primitive tribes, rarely deal in any systematic fashion with that pervasive Judeo-Christian *matière* that constituted until recently the core of most Western culture. In any case, I was permitted to get through school with an irresponsibly casual acquaintance with the Bible; and my conversations with students and colleagues have not persuaded me that my own experience was unique.[1]

Ziolkowski suggests that this cultural revolution presents formidable problems for rhetorical and historical criticism. Perceiving scriptural texts in a writer of Conrad's ilk is a minor obstacle that can be gotten over by carefully attending to the Bible and to the details of Conrad's fiction. Hearing the texts as a writer like Conrad might have intended them to be heard is far more challenging. For most of us, as Ziolkowski points out, Scripture has been neutralized. We are detached from it to a degree that Conrad and his readers surely were not. For the *bibelfest* generations, Scripture was freighted with layers of emotional significance. So intimate was their acquaintance with the Bible that one

---

[1] Theodore Ziolkowski, *Fictional Transfigurations of Jesus,* p. ix.

suspects that they would have answered Lingard's question without taking thought. Of course, then, our detachment has its gains, if we have leaped over the minor obstacle. Taking thought, we in our turn can appreciate Conrad in ways many of his first readers could not.

Yet critics of modernist literature often do not see that first small obstacle. We like to think that modernists are one of us, that we share their prejudices. The critic of Shakespeare or Milton, Johnson or Swift cannot be so deceived. We expect scriptural rhetoric from them, and we find it. Except for obvious cases like Joyce and Eliot, however, we are inclined to forget that modernists who grew up in the nineteenth century and flourished in the twentieth had assimilated the Bible as thoroughly as Carlyle or Ruskin or Shakespeare. Those modernists regarded Scripture as a part of the language of the tribe. We forget that at our peril.

Yeats and criticism of Yeats furnish examples. I have from time to time tried to keep up with Yeats criticism, and I have not seen a close study of Yeats's borrowings from the Bible. No one, so far as I know, has recognized that "Innisfree" begins with a very common Old Testament locution, meant, I suppose, to establish the poem's sense of placid security. We shall see that Conrad uses it, too, though not for Yeats's purpose. "On a Political Prisoner" supplies an amazing example of the limits of our late-twentieth-century eyes. Of Con, Yeats writes, "Blind and leader of the blind / Drinking the foul ditch where they lie" (lines 11–12). The pun is evidently far more apparent than the allusion. Puzzled by the image of the blind person in the ditch, T. R. Henn, an able detector of allusions, resorts to the circular game that Yeats encourages, referring us to a passage in Yeats's *Upanishads*. The equally skilled Norman Jeffares sends us to Yeats's use of the same image in "A Dialogue of Self and Soul."[2] They illustrate Ziolkowski's observation. It is mildly astonishing that neither critic knows the text in Matthew: "Let them alone; they be blind leaders of the blind. And if the blind lead the blind, both shall fall into the ditch" (15:14). Thus Yeats makes Con a Pharisee, the allusion amplifying the disdain he preferred not to state outright.

Of course, modernists characteristically prefer not to state outright. Their scriptures are so displaced or disguised that they can be readily missed. In this wise Conrad departs from most modernists, as one might expect. For that reason, perhaps, Conrad criticism, unlike Yeats criticism, has not ignored his fondness for scriptural metaphors. There have been more than a dozen notices, to be cited in due course, of Conrad's uses of Scripture. I cannot pretend that merely pointing out Conrad's debt to the Bible is an original contribution. No one, however, has suspected how extensive was Conrad's indebtedness. The reader innocent of Scripture can grasp a good deal of Conrad well enough. I will show, however, that we miss much in *The Secret Agent* if we miss its dominant scriptural metaphors. An understanding of the workings of Scripture in *Under Western Eyes,* *Chance,* and *The Rescue* is even more vital to seeing their designs. And for those who do not see its scriptures, its titular allusion in particular, *Victory* must remain a blank wall. My thesis is that, through *The Secret Agent,* scriptural allusion whether as metaphor or as mixed metaphor tends to retain its normative status. With *Under Western Eyes,* Conrad begins to turn to parody, a parody that becomes increasingly blatant as he writes his way through *The Res-*

---

[2]T. R. Henn, *The Lonely Tower,* p. 97; Norman Jeffares, *A Commentary on the Collected Poems of W. B. Yeats,* p. 232.

cue. Furthermore, I work out a new conception of Conrad's career, arguing that, by generally accepted aesthetic criteria, Conrad's later work signifies not a decline in his artistic powers but, in some ways, an increase. What declines in later Conrad is his moral imagination. Nothing could be more mistaken than the decline theorists' idea that the world of later Conrad is a place of flowers and blessings, a flight from the horror of nihilism. On the contrary, *Chance, Victory,* and *The Rescue* imitate Gulliver in the stable, thoroughly drenched in a hate of the human. Those works deride all traditional structures and values. Seen with one eye, they can be very funny books. Seen with both, they are morally repellent.

Those arguments develop throughout this book. My method of organization, focusing on biblical texts rather than on Conrad's fiction, requires some patience before the whole argument falls into place—I hope convincingly. Chapter 2 treats a subject that Conrad habitually addresses through the dark glass of Scripture: writing. Conrad's aesthetic stated and implied is so shot through with scriptural metaphors that a work like the famous Preface to *The Nigger of the "Narcissus"* could be easily mistaken for a tract on art for Christ's sake. But his purposes are rhetorical, not spiritual. Chapter 3 treats Conrad's handling of some Old Testament commonplaces that everyone knows, but he transforms to fashion his idiosyncratic vision of history. The fourth chapter takes up one of Conrad's favorite Old Testament stories, the saga of Moses and the Exodus. It also contributes to his idea of history. The Gospels are the subject of my fifth chapter. They have a peculiar standing in Conrad, retaining their normative value throughout his career. The sixth chapter considers last things, Conrad's addiction throughout his career to apocalyptic texts in the Gospels, the Epistles, and Revelation. We end, then, with the thief in the night.

It should not be surprising that Conrad relies upon the English Bible. Coming from the outside to the traditions of English literature, Conrad must have been quick to realize that scriptural metaphor is one of its distinctive traits, that the King James Bible was a seminal artifact of the culture. To become an English writer in the last quarter of the nineteenth century meant making the English Bible his own. Moreover, Conrad came from a literary tradition that prized Scripture as much as does English literature, Polish romanticism. The romantics' historiosophy was rooted in biblical prefigurations. His father was one of its last adherents.[3] In the English Bible, Conrad found a way to join his old world to his new.

Abundant though the evidence is in the fiction that Conrad read and reread the King James Bible with great care, he never takes an epigraph from it for a novel (save once, indirectly), and he never explicitly mentions reading the Bible in his letters or essays. Unfortunately, our only external evidence for what Conrad owed to the Bible comes from a source impossible to trust without several grains of salt, Ford Madox Ford. In his defense, it is much to Ford's

[3]The best surveys in English of the Polish romantic movement are Czesław Miłosz, *The History of Polish Literature*, pp. 200–63; and Hans Kohn, *Pan-Slavism*, 2d ed., rev., pp. 29–53. Both offer detailed discussions of the romantics' messianic historiosophy. One primary document of the movement accessible to the non-Polish reader is Josef Marie Hoene-Wronski, *Philosophie absolue de l'histoire*. His thesis is that Poland will be liberated "according to the promises of the Messiah," but the work is far more intelligent than that bare thesis suggests. On Conrad's father see Czesław Miłosz, "Apollo Korzeniowski: Joseph Conrad's Father," *Mosaic* 6 (1972): 121–40; Gustav Morf, *The Polish Shades and Ghosts of Joseph Conrad*, pp. 3–53; and Frederick R. Karl, *Joseph Conrad: The Three Lives*, pp. 14–125.

credit that on more than one occasion he argued that the fruitful question to ask about Conrad's style is not why Conrad did not write in French but how he learned to write in English. One of those occasions is in *A Personal Remembrance*, and in the course of his argument Ford retails a delightful anecdote from, so he says, Conrad on his Lowestoft days:

He once or twice said that going down Ratcliffe Highway he was jumped out at from a doorway by a gentleman who presented him with a pocket copy of the English Bible. This was printed on rice paper. He used the leaves for rolling cigarettes, but before smoking always read the page. So, he said, he learned English. The writer has always imagined this story to be one of Conrad's mystifications.[4]

Whose mystification? Ford's demur is almost enough to credit the truth that Conrad told the story. But it would not be beyond Ford to add the demur for that reason. At any rate, even if the jumping gentleman existed, even if Conrad sacrificed Scripture to vice, Conrad came by another copy that did not go up in smoke. Not in that way, at least.

[4] Ford Madox Ford, *Joseph Conrad: A Personal Remembrance*, p. 96.

WRESTLING WITH THE LORD

One subject that usually provokes Conrad to Scripture is writing. Whether appreciating the work of others, describing his own imaginative experience, or wrestling with theory, Conrad turns for his metaphors to the English Bible. Sometimes he uses Scripture to cover his tracks, the readymade phrases substituting for analysis. Sometimes, most obviously in his reviews, Scripture is made to serve a jocular English tone. But I can imagine more fundamental motives. For one, Conrad's penchant for biblical allusion may testify to the essential truth of Ford's smoking anecdote: the act of writing may have been so intimately linked in Conrad's mind with reading the English Bible that its rhythms and images readily come out when writing is his theme. For another, perhaps only in the Bible could Conrad find metaphors of commitment equal to his own. His scriptural metaphors for writing do not imply a theory of the religion of art. Nor are they meant to suggest that art can be a surrogate for the religious experience. They certainly are not meant to advocate a Christian idea of the temporal and spiritual functions of art. Rather, Conrad resorts to scriptural metaphor when writing is his theme because he feels as awed by the mystery of art as Paul by the mystery of Christ. When, in the Preface to *The Nigger of the "Narcissus,"* Conrad evangelizes, avowing that the artist speaks to "the sense of mystery surrounding our lives . . . to the latent feeling of fellowship with all creation," and that, in that most holy of phrases, his task "is, before all, to make you *see*," Paul inspires him: "And to make all men see what is the fellowship of the mystery, which from the beginning of the world hath been hid in God, who created all things by Jesus Christ" (Eph. 3:9). Paul inspires because in such a text Conrad finds an adequate figure for the emotions provoked when he recollects the experience of making art.

Solemnity is not in fashion when Conrad reviews the work of others in the essays collected in *Notes on Life and Letters.* There Scripture is distorted or used as mixed metaphor to raise a smile.

A passage in the essay on Anatole France provides a nice example. When Conrad hopes that France's political philosophy will not contaminate his art, he summons up Luke and Solomon. France, he writes "may be able . . . to forget that the evils are many and the remedies are few . . . because love is stronger than truth" (p. 38). The first allusion is a mixed metaphor, the second a silent, whimsical distortion of the text. The original for the second gives "death" for Conrad's "truth" and offers a more restrained simile: "Love is as strong as death" (Song of Sol. 8:6). That Conrad knowingly subverts the text we can assume from his other use of the phrase, in *The Mirror of the Sea:* "Love, though in a sense it may be admitted to be stronger than death, is by no means so universal and so sure" (p. 25). The substitution freights "truth" with irony, for the "truth" he hopes

France will forget is "that there is no universal panacea, that fatality is invincible; that there is an implacable menace of death in the triumph of the humanitarian idea." Thus the first allusion quietly exemplifies the point that humanitarian ideas always die. Conrad twists Jesus' words to the seventy apostles, "The harvest truly is great, but the labourers are few" (Luke 10:2; cf. Matt. 9:37–38). We shall see later that Conrad is fond of these chapters. Here his mixed text suggests that the dream of universal socialism will go the way of the dream of universal Christianity. Conrad phrases this theme far more somberly in *Nostromo* when Mrs. Gould thinks that "there was something inherent in the necessities of successful action which carried with it the moral degradation of the idea" (p. 521). But here the wit of allusion lightens the theme.

The wit of allusion works, too, in Conrad's review of *The Ascending Effort,* a tract urging art to preach the gospel of science. There Conrad pricks the pretensions of science and of H. G. Wells, "an awesome, august voice, like the voice of Judgement Day; a great voice, perhaps the voice of science itself, uttering the words: 'There shall be no more pain!'" (p. 73). Conrad alludes to the vision of the New Jerusalem in Revelation: "And I heard a great voice out of heaven saying, Behold, the tabernacle of God is with man . . . . And God shall wipe away all tears from their eyes; and there shall be no more death, . . . neither shall there be any more pain: for the former things are passed away" (21:3–4). The same text is used to provoke pathos (or scorn) at Lena's death in *Victory* (p. 405), and Conrad often resorts to it or to parallel passages in Revelation. In "The Ascending Effort" Conrad employs it at Wells's expense to say that Wells's alliance of science and art will not lead us to the new heaven and new earth.

13

Maupassant is quite another voice, "The voice of one crying in the wilderness, Prepare ye the way of the Lord, make his paths straight" (Matt. 3:3). Maupassant's way, however, is "the integrity of an art [that] will let none of the fascinations that beset a writer working in loneliness turn him away from the straight path, from the vouchsafed vision of excellence" (p. 26). Conrad extends the metaphor delightfully through another text. Writes Conrad, "No tempting demon has ever succeeded in hurling him down from his high, if narrow, pedestal" (p. 27). The relevant text is either *Paradise Regained* or its source, Matthew's description of the temptation in the wilderness: "Then the devil taketh him up into the holy city, And setteth him on a pinnacle of the temple, And saith unto him, If thou be the Son of God, cast thyself down" (Matt. 4:5–6). We are asked, apparently, to alter Jesus' reply to read, "Thou shalt not tempt the Lord thy Maupassant." Although Conrad seems to be lavishing praise upon Maupassant, the wry allusion says something else. Perhaps it reveals anxieties of influence.

These allusions amuse, and that seems their chief function, a method in public essays of creating a jocular "English" voice. But they also help Conrad evade analytical problems, most obviously in the essay on Maupassant, where Conrad uses them to dodge analytical thinking about the dynamics of imagination. Perhaps the last two sentences of the Maupassant essay contain a drop of self-criticism: "This creative artist has the true imagination: he never condescends to invent anything; he sets up no empty pretenses. And he stoops to no littleness in his art— least of all to the miserable vanity of a catching phrase" (p. 31).

One senses less of that vanity in Conrad's letters when he

14

bewails impasses or celebrates triumphs in his own writing. Consistently Conrad likens bouts of creative impotence to crucifixion, success or hope of it to resurrection—and for the most part seriously, without irony or humor. Of "The Rescuer" Conrad writes Garnett (February 7, 1897) that it "sleeps yet the sleep like of death," and asks, "Will there be a miracle and a resurrection?"[1] Four months later (June 11, 1897), his struggles with that novel prompt an allusion out of Luke (23:39) that Conrad would use again writing Cunninghame Graham: "But generally I feel like the impenitent thief on the cross (he is one of my early heroes)—defiant and bitter."[2] Two years later Conrad is still crucified upon "The Rescuer." Heading his letter "Good Friday 1899" and writing under that, "in sorrow and tribulation," Conrad wails: "There is not a spark left in me. I am overwhelmed and utterly flattened."[3] Success, however, is salvation, resurrection. For example, Conrad writes William Rothenstein (June 27, 1904), "I am not myself and shall not be myself till I am born again after *Nostromo* is finished" (see John 3:3-7); to E. V. Lucas (June 23, 1909), about recovering from the fear that his "writing life seems to [have] come to an end," Conrad asks, "But how long these resurrections will go on, who can tell?"[4]

Conrad's psychoanalytical biographer, Bernard Meyer, has allowed that "there is some reason to suspect an identification of himself with Jesus."[5] I suppose that passages like these could support Meyer. But there is nothing excep-

[1] Joseph Conrad, *Letters from Joseph Conrad, 1895-1924*, ed. Edward Garnett, pp. 88-89.
[2] Ibid., p. 98; Joseph Conrad, *Joseph Conrad's Letters to Cunninghame Graham*, ed. C. T. Watts, pp. 59 and 62n.
[3] Conrad, *Letters*, ed. Garnett, p. 152.
[4] G. Jean-Aubry, *Joseph Conrad: Life and Letters*, 1:330, 2:100.
[5] Bernard Meyer, *Joseph Conrad: A Psychoanalytic Biography*, p. 352.

15

tional about an artist exposed in childhood to a mystical variety of Catholicism deriving from the Passion his metaphors for the sorrows and tribulations of writing. These passages probably say more about Conrad's intense commitment to his craft than they do about "a deep and abiding devotion to that early Catholic faith."[6] Perhaps only the Passion could provide Conrad with metaphors strong enough to describe his struggles with the word. In his essay on James, Conrad imagines an artist at the world's end speaking out because "he is so much of a voice that, for him, silence is like death" (*Notes,* p. 14). Writing for Conrad was a type of revelation, a type of theophany.

Theophany is the theme of Conrad's memorable account, in *A Personal Record,* of writing *Nostromo:*

All I know is that, for twenty months, neglecting the common joys of life that fall to the lot of the humblest of this earth, I had, like the prophet of old, "wrestled with the Lord" for my creation, for the headlands of the coast, for the darkness of the Placid Gulf, the light on the snows, the clouds on the sky, and for the breath of life that had to be blown into the shapes of men and women, of Latin and Saxon, of Jew and Gentile.[P. 98]

The second allusion is, of course, to the second account of creation in Genesis: "And the Lord God formed man of the dust of the ground, and breathed into his nostrils the breath of life; and man became a living soul" (Gen. 2:7). Avrom Fleishman remarks that Conrad's language here "subtly modifies the traditional metaphor of the artist in the image of God, and makes him specifically the creator of a historical world."[7] The trinity of pairs at the close certainly gives that impression: the creatures of Conrad's making have distinc-

---

[6] Ibid., p. 351.
[7] Avrom Fleishman, *Conrad's Politics,* p. 161.

tive sexual, racial, and religious origins, origins linked to
and modified by the natural environment of coast, Gulf,
mountains, and sky. And the point of the first allusion is
precisely that the world Conrad makes is historical. Jacob is
the "prophet" who, at the ford Jabbok, wrestles with god
and is transformed from the wily trickster of Isaac and
Laban to the holy patriarch, from Jacob to Israel: "Thy
name shall be called no more Jacob, but Israel: for as a
prince hast thou power with God and with men, and hast
prevailed" (Gen. 32:28). When Jacob becomes Israel, history
begins. The artist, the analogy says, is not merely made "in
the image of God." He has prevailed like Jacob. Hence Conrad concludes, "These are, perhaps, strong words" (p. 98).

I know of only one other explicit allusion to Jacob in
Conrad's work, that in the potboiler "A Smile of Fortune."
Conrad may have stuck it in to amuse himself. It is a non-
sensical mixed metaphor that has nothing to do with the
tale. But that may caution us against taking too solemnly
that Jacob allusion in *A Personal Record.*

In the tale the young Captain's first encounter with
Jacobus, the ship chandler, parodies Jacob's deception of
Isaac (Gen. 27). At Rebekah's urging, Jacob gets "two good
kids of goats" to masquerade as the "savoury meat" of veni-
son that Isaac has bid Esau kill and cook for him, thence
to receive Isaac's blessing. But dressed in hairy skins so as
to pass for his brother when the blind Isaac touches him,
Jacob gives the goat meat to Isaac, tricks him, and receives
the blessing in Esau's stead. When Jacobus visits the young
Captain with a splendid breakfast, he plays Jacob to the
Captain's Isaac. Looking at the meat, the Captain exclaims,
"'Are these goat cutlets?'" but the steward assures him that
they are "'real mutton.'" The Captain has mistaken Alfred
Jacobus for his brother, Ernest, with whom his owners had

17

instructed him to deal. Like Jacob, Alfred comes beforehand to get the Captain's business. Unlike Isaac, though, the Captain is undeceived, and the more galled for it: "'I had the sense of having been circumvented somehow. Yet I had deceived myself'" ("Smile," pp. 9–12).

Unless we are supposed to hear in Jacobus's maneuvers to marry the Captain to his illegitimate daughter an echo of Laban and Leah, the allusion is never developed, and it does nothing to clear away the confusions of a piece written for cash.[8] The parody is a private joke, no more. Thus it might be wise not to make too much of Conrad's "strong words" in *A Personal Record* about besting God.

Jacob's wrestling could, however, have had private significance for Conrad, similarly transformed from seaman to writer, from Joseph Korzeniowski to Joseph Conrad. Moreover, the allusion may tell us how to see a peculiarity of Conrad's plot in *Nostromo* and in other fictions, the plot he uses, in fact, in *A Personal Record*. There are in *Nostromo* three sudden, apparently arational, and manifestly parallel transformations of character—conversions—and each has pestered critics. They befall the three men who suffer the night journey on the Placid Gulf. Nostromo returns overwhelmed by an impression of betrayal that eventually kills him. Decoud, remaining on Great Isabel, allows his isolation to overwhelm him, and he kills himself. Finally, the Jewish trader, Hirsch, who has been overwhelmed by horrid fears of physical pain, miraculously transforms himself from a coward to a gallant man, spitting defiantly at his torturer, who then shoots him. Mimetic explanations of these conversions cannot satisfy. Conrad, I suspect, imitates a biblical conception of plot, a conception that flogs realism

---

[8]Lawrence Graver, *Conrad's Short Fiction*, p. 159.

to the end of illustrating how the holy enters into history. Jacob the trickster becomes Israel. Moses, not unlike Hirsch, flees Egypt for fear of his life, meets God in a strange land, and becomes the leader of Israel. Jesus becomes Christ. Saul becomes Paul. Nostromo, Decoud, and Hirsch take another road to Damascus. So does Willems, in *An Outcast of the Islands,* transformed from a cowardly domestic tyrant and a thief to a demon lover who upsets a kingdom, and back again. More provocative are the mysteries of conversion that visit Kurtz and Marlow in *Heart of Darkness,* Jim in *Lord Jim,* Comrade Ossipon in *The Secret Agent,* Razumov in *Under Western Eyes,* Heyst and Lena in *Victory.* These varieties of conversion in Conrad's fiction may be owing to a lifelong intimacy with biblical literature. At any rate, Jacob's wrestling resumes a fundamental peculiarity of Conrad's art, radical discontinuity. In Conrad theophany is secularized, meant to elucidate not the workings of God in history but the workings of the arational fatalities that always threaten to overwhelm the dailiness of life, the placid surface of historical existence. Yet the sacred model straddles Conrad's secular worlds like a distended shadow, like a vision reflected darkly in a glass.

Of course, the plot of dazzling conversion is common in the literature of religious cultures. Conrad might have acquired it as readily from reading Greek drama and epic as from the Bible. Or he could have picked it up from Shakespeare, and thus secondhand from Scripture. But the scenes of conversion in Conrad bear such marked similarities to Jacob's wrestling as to make it the likely source. It can hardly be coincidental that episodes of physical wrestling normally precede Conrad's conversions. Lena grapples with Ricardo. Marlow, at midnight, struggles by a riverbank with the ghastly body and soul of Mr. Kurtz (pp. 140–

19

43). Jim meets Gentleman Brown by the ford of a creek in a "contest" that the dying Brown likens to wrestling, shaking Jim's "'two-penny soul around and inside out and upside down—by God!'" (p. 384). Ossipon grapples with Winnie Verloc, dressed in mourning, in the darkened shop of shady wares, her late husband's corpse for witness (p. 291). Most terrible of all is Razumov's wrestling in the darkened stairwell with Nikita and his henchmen (pp. 368–69). In each episode setting, mood, and action recapitulate the strange terror of Jacob's dark wrestling with God at the ford Jabbok. After each, conversion comes. Although I can detect in these scenes no verbal echoes of the trickster's conversion in Genesis, the dramatic similarities are so striking and the repetition of the motif so persistent that I am inclined to think that Conrad fashioned these scenes on the biblical pattern. Its shadow prevails.

The significance of the Jacob allusion in *A Personal Record* seems to have been evident to Ford. He too finds it a metaphor for miraculous conversion. After he relates the anecdote about the biblical gentleman who accosted Conrad on the highway, Ford says of Conrad, "What is miraculous is that he took English, as it were, by the throat and, wrestling till the dawn, made it obedient to him as it had been obedient to few other men."[9]

When he considers theory of fiction, Conrad unearths tellurian metaphors. Borrowing from Genesis again in "Books," Conrad takes the traditional world-making analogy: "Every novelist must begin by creating for himself a world, great or little, in which he can honestly believe. This world cannot be made otherwise than in his own image" (*Notes*, p. 6;

[9] Ford Madox Ford, *Joseph Conrad: A Personal Remembrance*, p. 109.

cf. Gen. 1:26–27). But he quickly abandons this cliché for a more original metaphor, a conflation of two beatitudes: "The novelist . . . is the chronicler of the adventures of mankind amongst the dangers of the kingdoms of the earth. And the kingdom of the earth itself, the ground on which his individuals stand, stumble, or die, must enter into his scheme of faithful record. To encompass all this is a great feat" (pp. 6–7). The justice of Fleishman's point is again apparent—the novelist a historian, a chronicler composing a faithful record. But one of the senses of the many-edged adjective suggests that the novelist's commitment is larger than the historian's, his record not only accurate but also written in a spirit akin to the prophet's: "And I took unto me faithful witnesses to record" (Isa. 8:2). Contrasting novelist and historian in his essay on Henry James, Conrad tries to define the object of the novelist's faith, again through an earthy metaphor. Fiction "stands on firmer ground" than history because "based on the reality of forms, . . . whereas history is based on documents, . . . on second-hand impression" (*Notes,* p. 17). Whatever Conrad may mean by "the reality of forms," the difference is one of degree rather than kind. The writer of fiction is closer to the earth and thus "nearer truth." Perhaps "the reality of forms" is identical to "the kingdom of the earth," and what this means we may see by contrast with its source: instead of "the kingdom of heaven," the novelist must "inherit the earth" (Matt. 5:3,5). Conrad's other notable use of this expression, out of the mouth of the Professor in *The Secret Agent,* indicates that Matthew is the source. The Professor rails against the "multitude" to whom Jesus preached the Sermon on the Mount, "the blind, . . . the deaf and dumb, . . . the halt and the lame," because "theirs is the kingdom of the earth" (p. 303). But in "Books," Conrad may have another text in mind, one that comes just before Matthew's rendition of the Sermon on the Mount, from the episode that furnishes Conrad with his jibe at Maupassant: "Again the devil taketh him up to an exceeding high mountain, and sheweth him all the kingdoms of the world" (Matt. 4:8). This text would make an even more daring metaphor than conflation of the two beatitudes, since it implies that the novelist must embrace what Jesus rejects. Whichever text, the argument is the same. The novelist has faith not in the hope of heaven but in the earth and history. Of the earth, earthy. Writing to Graham, Conrad says of novelists who write copiously and well, "Of such . . . is the kingdom of the Earth."[10]

In his essay on John Galsworthy, Conrad claims the earth again, now with an eye on another provocative text: "And to be tied to the earth (even as the hewers of wood and drawers of water are tied to the earth) in the exercise of one's imagination, by every scruple of conscience and honor, may be considered a lot hard enough not to be lightly embraced. This is why novelists are comparatively rare" (*Last Essays*, p. 126). Again, fiction is a type of history. In the essay Conrad contrasts fiction with fairy tales. By fairy tale he means any work that, in the "pride of fanciful invention, . . . soars (on goose's wings) into the empty blue" (p. 126). Against such visionary flights the writer of fiction is "a single-minded observer and conscientious interpreter of reality." As he does elsewhere—at the end of the Maupassant essay, for example—Conrad distinguishes between invention and imagination, symbolic and metaphorical thinking. The inventor creates from nothing and goes, Conrad's avian image suggests, to nothing. The imaging

[10]Conrad, *Letters*, ed. Watts, p. 129, letter of January 4, 1900.

novelist observes what is and interprets it, puts sensations into words.

The hewers and drawers of Conrad's metaphor are the Gibeonites who saved their skins by a ruse (Josh. 9). When the Gibeonites observe that the Hebrews mean to slaughter all the natives of the Promised Land, they "work wilily," outfitting themselves as if come from another country to make alliance with the Hebrews in the name of "the Lord thy God." The ruse discovered after the alliance has been sworn, Joshua condemns the Gibeonites to perpetual slavery, "hewers of wood and drawers of water for the house of my God."

In its context Conrad's allusion emphasizes the rhetoric of fiction, the novelist's ties to the reality of forms and to the readers of the earth. And the writer of fiction, though rare, is, like the Gibeonites, not one of the chosen of the Lord. He survives on sufferance, by virtue of his ruses. Working wilily, Conrad grafts on another allusion in case we have missed his point, a revision of a passage from the Preface to *The Nigger of the "Narcissus"*: the fairy tale "in its various disguises . . . will always be with us," like the poor of Jesus' saying (Matt. 26:11). Like Jesus, the novelist we will not always have among us.

The allusions are, however, a Gibeonite ruse, outfits of a far country meant to cover up evasions of vexing philosophical problems. What is invention's source? How does one observe? How interpret? How does one proceed from observing to interpreting? And what is this "reality" observed and interpreted? Instead of answers, Conrad supplies neat pairs of question-begging epithets—air and earth, pride and conscience, irresponsibility and conscientiousness, playing and working—and resonant allusions.

23

Yet the central argument is clear enough: fiction allies itself with surviving, by whatever ruses the situation requires, amid the dangers of the historical world. Conrad is concerned not with theory of fiction but with theory colored by his own experience of imagining fiction. "Fiction," he says in *A Personal Record,* "is but truth often dragged out of a well and clothed in the painted robe of imaged phrases" (p. 93). The writer of fiction, unlike the historian or the teller of fairy tales, revises Genesis, hauling Joseph from the well, mending his tattered coat of many colors (Gen. 37:23–24).

It is in this spirit that we might best approach the Preface to *The Nigger of the "Narcissus."* Cast upon it a cold philosophical eye, it withers.[11] Gaze upon it as "an inward account of [Conrad's] creative aspiration,"[12] it becomes Joseph the dreamer retailored, but, strangely, not in the earthy habiliments that Conrad usually assumes. I am uneasy with the claim that "there is nothing in the Preface which is contradicted in Conrad's later criticism."[13] The earthy emphasis of "Books" and of "John Galsworthy" is not that of the Preface. There Conrad takes wing. With very few traces of irony Conrad appears to advocate a purer form of Christian art, his sentiments stitched together with extracts from some of the more mystical passages of the New Testament, his symbolism derived from the Mass.

Memories of a Roman Catholic childhood surely linger in Conrad's description of the task of art:

[11] David Goldknopf, *The Life of the Novel,* pp. 82–83, casts the coldest eye.

[12] Ian Watt, "Conrad's Preface to *The Nigger of the 'Narcissus,'"* *Novel* (Winter, 1974):103.

[13] Ibid., p. 115.

The task approached in tenderness and faith is to hold up un-
questioningly, without choice and without fear, the rescued fragment before all eyes in the light of a sincere mood . . . [to]
reveal the substance of its truth—disclose its inspiring secret:
the stress and passion within the core of each convincing moment . . . [to] awaken in the hearts of the beholders that feeling
of unavoidable solidarity. [Preface, p. xxvi]

Holding up a rescued fragment in a mood inspired by faith,
the artist is like unto the priest at the Offertory holding
up the consecrated host at the moment of transubstantiation, reenacting the Passion and the Resurrection, making
the beholders one body in Christ. This is the most Joycean
passage in Conrad, reminiscent of the boy in "Araby" bearing his chalice through the crowded streets. But Conrad's
description is without irony, like the references to passion
and resurrection in his letters. He seems to be seriously
asking us to partake of the holy communion of art.

This symbolism is of a piece with the scriptures of the
Preface. The whipping boy of the Galsworthy essay is the
fairy tale. In the Preface it is science, and Conrad whips
it to make claims for the permanence of art: "Its effect
endures forever. The changing wisdom of successive generations discards ideas, questions facts, demolishes theories.
But the artist appeals to that part of our being which is
not dependent on wisdom; to that in us which is a gift and
not an acquisition—and therefore more permanently en-
during" (p. xxiv). That mysterious part of our being, given,
not acquired, echoes the Collect for the day in the Preface,
from Ephesians. Conrad has in mind an analogy with the
gift of grace. Paul writes: "For by grace are ye saved through
faith; and that not of yourselves: it is the gift of God" (Eph.
2:8). The notion that art's "effect endures forever" rehearses

another epistolary text that pits the changing against the permanent: "For all flesh is as grass, and all the glory of man as the flower of the grass. The grass withereth, and the flower thereof falleth away: But the word of the Lord endureth for ever" (1 Pet. 1:24–25). Art, then, endures not because it is rooted in the earth and bound up in history but because it appeals to some noncontingent, ahistorical capacity in us to receive truth.

That art endures is one of the four articles of faith Conrad offers. The others are that art imparts truth, that fellowship makes this truth efficacious, and that the final cause of endurance, truth, and solidarity is the artist's power to exercise our spiritual eye. The word "truth" appears ten times in Conrad's brief discourse, opening and ending the essay. Art is "bringing to light the truth." This truth is unitary, not plural. Art tries to find "the one illuminating and convincing quality—the very truth." When the attempt succeeds, "all the truth of life is there." Conrad's uses smack more of Christianity than of Platonism. "Truth dwells" in Conrad's confession of belief in solidarity; "the truth" of art "should abide" with the true artist "as the most precious of his possessions." This inward and personal conception imitates "the truth . . . which dwelleth in us, and shall be with us for ever" and "the Spirit of truth" which will "abide with you for ever" (2 John 2; John 14:16–17). The inward truth for John or for Conrad is that which alone endures, untouched by the vicissitudes of history.

Like truth, "solidarity" or "fellowship" is also inward, a "latent feeling" of "mysterious origin," "a mystery surrounding our lives . . . that knits together the loneliness of innumerable hearts," that "in toil, in joy, in hope . . . binds men to each other" (pp. xxiv, xxvi). Again Conrad practices the imitation of Paul: "Now the God of hope fill you with all joy . . . that ye may abound in hope"; "being knit together in love . . . to the acknowledgement of the mystery of God" (Rom. 15:13; Col. 2:2-3). For fellowship's sake, Conrad goes so far as to imagine himself delivering another Sermon on the Mount, he the spokesman for "the disregarded multitude of the bewildered, the simple and the voiceless" (p. xxiv)—the multitudes of the poor in spirit, the poor in heart, the meek (Matt. 5:1-8). Here we might smell earth again, "the salt of the earth" (Matt. 5:13), but Conrad's intonations are more mystical than that. His "solidarity" or "fellowship" does not denote a political or historical conception. It is spiritual, an "avowal" of faith. Like Paul, Conrad insists that he shows us a mystery.

Indeed, there is in the Preface what a heretic has called a "somewhat obsessive emphasis on the optical process."[14] A source of this obsession is those New Testament texts far more obsessed than Conrad with distinguishing between seeing with the flesh and seeing with the spirit, between perception and insight. The latter sense is on Conrad's mind when he swears that his "task . . . is, by the power of the written word to make you hear, to make you feel—it is, before all, to make you *see*" (p. xxvi). Italics aside, the intriguing word is, as Watt remarks, the infinitive "make."[15] Watt finds in the word a clue to the narrative strategies in Conrad's fiction. I am more impressed by its ring of authority, by the yen for compulsion that it connotes.

The masterful array of rhetorical appeals in the Preface makes it deserving of its fame. As befits a discourse arguing that art's "high desire is to reach the secret spring of responsive emotions" (p. xxv), it varies its tone, alternately

14 Goldknopf, *Life*, p. 83.
15 Watt, "Conrad's Preface," p. 109.

humble, avuncular, and proud. Like Kurtz, it has its fill of the emotions. Conrad begins humbly enough, using the word in his first sentence. He is humble too in his repetitions of the words "attempt," "try," and the like. He is humble in his avowal of "tenderness and faith." As he moves toward his close, Conrad turns amiable, a good-humored soul who makes scriptural jokes about "sentimentalism"—"like the poor, . . . exceedingly difficult to get rid of"—and, introducing the plural pronoun, stretches out with us beneath a tree watching the motions of a laborer in the distance. In the last paragraph, he becomes the weary seer: "a moment of vision, a sigh, a smile—and the return to eternal rest" (p. xxviii). Yet a mixture of pride and pathos dominates the piece. The third paragraph begins with the artist-hero plunging for our sakes "into that lonely region of stress and strife." The sixth calls out for tears, describing the "sincere endeavour" of the artist going "as far on that road as his strength will carry him, . . . undeterred by faltering, weariness or reproach." And this concerto of appeals works. We are moved. We cry. The fame of the Preface is witness.

The most masterful passage of them all is "to make you see." Humility first: the "task" is one that Conrad is only "trying to achieve." With the authoritative "make," however, Conrad begins to bully us. Now the first-person singular rules, speaking to a wretched "you" who, bereft of the "power" of the first person's writing, cannot hear, feel, or see. What "I" will ultimately make "you" see, providing "you" deserve it ("according to your deserts"), is "that glimpse of truth for which you have forgotten to ask." For this wretched "you" there Conrad goes too far. The clause insults me. The reader who would forget to ask for truth would never pick up the Preface in the first place. The clause is startlingly revealing of Conrad's conception of his reader, of the great gulf fixed between that reader and the author of the Preface, in despite of "solidarity." The voice is a true believer's to the heathen. Conrad is as sure as Paul that he has the power of "truth."

Paul's Epistles are, of course, notable for the same mastery of emotional appeals, for the same variety. And in the original of Conrad's passage, one finds a similar transition from humility to pride: "Unto me, who am less than the least of all saints, is this grace given, that I should preach among the Gentiles the unsearchable riches of Christ; And to make all men see what is the fellowship of the mystery, which from the beginning of the world hath been hid in God, who created all things by Jesus Christ" (Eph. 3:8–9). In a letter to Garnett (November 8, 1906), Conrad mentions his "theory of preaching to the Gentiles in the market place."[16] He does not explain himself, but the Preface plainly puts that theory in practice. Conrad has absorbed Pauline phrases and Pauline rhetoric, exaggerating the rhetoric. Paul's humility strikes me as far more appropriate and his pride far less offensive than Conrad's. There is seldom in Paul the immense distance between writer and reader that Conrad in the Preface sometimes assumes. Conrad's implied reader in the marketplace worships science and other abominations. Perhaps that imagined opposition is to blame for the rhetorical excesses and symbolic flights.

I do not suppose that Conrad is really advocating a purer form of Christian art. Except for the joke at sentimentalism's expense (and at the last I find the bonhomme Conrad harder to bear than the Conrad Tyrannus), the allusions to Scripture in the Preface seem unstudied, present thoughts, made

16Conrad, *Letters,* ed. Garnett, p. 199.

of a different stuff from Jacob's wrestling, Joseph's coat, and the hewers of wood. The allusions in the Preface lack that metaphorical specificity. They seem spontaneous reponses to the emotional pressures wrought on Conrad by his theme. If that impression is just, then the spontaneous, naïve quality of the allusions in the Preface would be evidence of Conrad's remarkable intimacy with the English Bible, an intimacy so fine that its phrases and rhetoric come unbidden at moments of emotional intensity. Conrad is not advocating Christian art. The tags from the New Testament come readily to him because in them he finds the only images adequate to embody his feelings about making art. Just as failures and successes call to Conrad's mind crucifixion and resurrection, so does the justification of fiction summon up evangelistic texts. Conrad's allusions in the Preface do not even presume to set up a religion of art. They are not species of logic. They are metaphors of feeling.

But perhaps I am mistaken about Conrad's image of his reader in the Preface. Perhaps, eight decades gone, Conrad might have reasonably assumed that his readers would easily detect his borrowings. The rhetoric of allusion is a rhetoric of solidarity. When Conrad talks of dragging truth from a well and dressing it in bright images, when he likens Wells to the great voice of Judgment or Maupassant to Jesus tempted, when he mentions the hewers of wood, when he compares writing *Nostromo* to a wrestling with God, then he invites his readers to join him in the fellowship of scriptural history. Readers in 1897 may have been gifted with such fine ears for Scripture that they could as easily hear the voice of Paul as the voice of Judgment Day. If so, then the allusions would not make gaps. They would mend them. Then Conrad's rhetoric would be consistent with this theme, and we would dispense with some of my objections to Conrad's tone.

For when Conrad writes about writing, he wants his scriptural allusions to identify him as an English writer. Those allusions are the language of the tribe. When Conrad writes about writing, allusions to the English Bible finally express a feeling other than a commitment to art. They express Conrad's yearning to be one of us—he too a Gibeonite, but one really from a far country, and dressed not in tattered clothes but in "imaged phrases" from the English Bible, another Joseph in a many-colored robe.

THE WRITING ON THE WALL

I have given up numbering Conrad's bows to Ecclesiastes, to the Book of Job, and to the first three chapters of Genesis. They are legion. Some of their number and Conrad's splendid revisions of the memorable event at King Belshazzar's feast are my subjects in this chapter. Out of these ordinary texts Conrad fashions an extraordinary symbolism that estranges us from conventional fields of thought. The reader unaware that these uses of Scripture have a history may be in the unhappy predicament of the astrologers at the feast.

Early and late, Conrad pays his respects to Ecclesiastes. In one of our first specimens of his English, a letter to Spiridion Kliszczewski (December 19, 1885), Conrad tries out the rhetoric of scriptural allusion with a gesture to the Preacher of vanity. Despairing of English political reforms, Conrad presumes to clinch an argument with the same device we have seen in the essays: "From above, I fear, we may obtain consolation, but no remedy. 'All is vanity.'"[1] The quotation

[1] G. Jean-Aubry, *Joseph Conrad: Life and Letters*, 1:85.

marks tell Kliszczewski that the writer knows what he is about, and they are consistent with the stilted language and thought of the letter—understandably stilted, of course. By the end of his life, Conrad has mastered the rhetoric of scriptural allusion, and much else, when he writes in "Travel" (1923): "But the time for such books of travel is past on this earth girt about with cables, with an atmosphere made restless by the waves of ether, lighted by that sun of the twentieth century under which there is nothing new left now, and but very little of what may be called obscure" (*Last Essays*, p. 88). In that fine sentence Conrad embeds two allusions, the first to his text for the *Nigger* Preface, the second to Ecclesiastes. His "earth girt about with cables" ironically imitates Paul's "having your loins girt about with truth" (Eph. 6:14), its irony signaling the reader to beware of the final clause, the obscurity. The second allusion imitates one of the refrains of Ecclesiastes (the Preacher uses it twenty-eight times), "under the sun," and Conrad bids us think specifically of the observation that "there is no new thing under the sun" (1:9). Famous though the phrase is, Conrad revises it so deftly that it barely obtrudes. He neither needs nor wants quotation marks now. And now, unlike the letter's pat allusion, Conrad manages the double vision that typifies his fictional scriptures, both following and departing from his source.

Significant revisions of texts from Ecclesiastes appear throughout Conrad, beginning with "Youth." James W. Mathews has heard some of the several biblical echoes in "Youth" and ably remarked their contribution to the meaning of the tale, "that the romantic vision brings only a temporary sense of achievement and then dejection."[2] One

---

[2]James W. Mathews, "Ironic Symbolism in Conrad's 'Youth,'" *SSF* 11 (1974):118.

likely allusion Mathews ignores, however, is that in the title and in Marlow's repeated apostrophes to "youth." The older Marlow acknowledges that "'youth, strength, genius, thoughts, achievements, simple hearts—all dies,'" yet yearns for youth's illusions of "'strength . . . faith . . . imagination'" (pp. 7, 12). If youth is "'ignorance,'" it is also "'hope'" (p. 18). The older Marlow's double vision brings the tale almost to its end: "'Only a moment; a moment of strength, of romance, of glamour—of youth! . . . A flick of sunshine upon a strange shore, the time to remember, the time for a sigh, and goodbye!—Night—Good-bye . . . !'" (p. 42). At the last Marlow works in the Preacher's list of times (Eccles. 3:1-8), so often mistaken for an affair fit for weddings. The Preacher's reductive wisdom that "all things come alike to all," that the swift and the strong must go the way of the halt and the weak, echoes in all of Marlow's apostrophes, and in all, too, the Preacher's advice to youth: "Rejoice, O young man, in thy youth; and let thy heart cheer thee in the days of thy youth, and walk in the ways of thine heart, and in the sight of thine eyes: but know thou, that for all these things God will bring thee to judgment" (11:9). As he does on two other occasions, Conrad identifies in his "Author's Note" to the *Youth* volume his controlling Scripture. Conrad says that he suspects Marlow "of some vanity—I don't mean in the Solomonian sense. Of all my people he's the one that has never been a vexation to my spirit" (p. xxviii). In the Preacher's wry ironies Conrad found a voice to follow all the days of his writing life. But his disillusionment is greater than the Preacher's, whose God of Judgment becomes Marlow's Night.

Jim is one youth who refuses to be disillusioned in this wise. We are alerted to that in the second paragraph of *Lord Jim*, when the opening narrator observes that "a water-clerk need not pass an examination in anything under the sun" (p. 3), the scripture a foretaste of Jim's intransigent vanity. Later, speaking of Jim's romance with Jewel, Marlow has it that one can understand "'the promptings of youth . . . unless one is incapable of understanding anything under the sun'" (p. 311). We should hear the Preacher reply that, when one applies one's "heart to know wisdom," one understands only "that a man cannot find out the work that is done under the sun" (8:16–17), that man is "incapable of understanding." Thus the allusion is a piece of dramatic irony, instructing us to doubt Marlow's wisdom.

Like Jim, the Professor of *The Secret Agent* is a preacher's son, and Scripture comes trippingly to his lips. Inviting Comrade Ossipon for beer at the Silenus, the "Perfect Anarchist" combines two scriptures in the saw "'Let us eat and drink, for tomorrow we die'" (p. 304). His second clause is found in Isaiah 22:13 and in 1 Corinthians 15:32: "let us eat and drink; for tomorrow we die." The prophet is damning the conduct of his people after the fall of Jerusalem; the evangelist, those who supplant God with Night, disbelieving in the resurrection of the dead. Luke, in a parable of a rich man who seeks material rewards alone, uses "eat, drink, and be merry" as a recipe for damnation (Luke 12:19), agreeing with Isaiah and Paul. The Preacher is, as usual where the redactors have not orthodoxed him, idiosyncratic, commending mirth as yet another example of the vanity of seeking for succor against the night: "because a man hath no better thing under the sun, than to eat, and to drink, and to be merry: for that shall abide with him of his labour the days of his life" (Eccles. 8:15). To the Professor, Ossipon gives the orthodox response: "'You be damned'" (p. 305). The Professor replies, in the spirit if not the letter of the Preacher, "'Let that be the hope of the weak, whose theology has invented hell for the strong.'" And again, "'Mankind does not know what it wants'" (p. 305). The preacher's son is Conrad's Preacher in *The Secret Agent.* Scorning revolutionary dreams, he asks, "'What's the good of thinking what will be?'" combining texts again. One text is the Preacher's question, ". . . for who can tell a man what shall be after him under the sun?" (6:12). In the other the Preacher answers himself and the Professor in a way that mocks the Professor's dedication to destroying "what is" so that the way can be prepared for "'a clean sweep and a new conception of life'" (pp. 73, 306). To what will be, the Preacher replies, of course, "The thing that hath been, it is that which shall be; and that which is done is that which shall be done: and there is no new thing under the sun" (1:9). Like the texts from Ecclesiastes in "Youth," those in *The Secret Agent* illustrate the tenacity of romantic illusions. Who more romantic than the Perfect Anarchist?

Possibly the millionaire. The great de Barral of *Chance* is the sum of vanity, of a "mediocrity" so "consistent" that "his very vanity seemed to miss the gratification of the mere show of power" (p. 84). For de Barral, despite his millions, "had gratified no tastes, had known no luxuries; he had built no gorgeous palaces, had formed no splendid galleries out of these 'immense sums'" (p. 84). The Preacher had sought the gratification that de Barral was too mediocre to entertain: "I made me great works; I builded me houses; I planted me vineyards. . . . And whatsoever mine eyes desired I kept not from them" (2:4-10). But de Barral seems to have learned the Preacher's moral, saying of his millions, "'What have I had out of them?'" (p. 84), just as, from his palaces and pleasures, the Preacher learns that "there was no profit under the sun" (2:11)—one of the many double-text jokes in which Conrad indulges.

The father of Axel Heyst is the Preacher's twin. What de Barral's mediocrity prevented the senior Heyst, "unhappy in a way unknown to mediocre souls," had done. Echoing the same text from Ecclesiastes that he uses in *Chance,* Conrad writes in *Victory* that "the elder Heyst had begun by coveting all the joys, those of the great and those of the humble, those of the fools and those of the sages," only, like the Preacher, to discover vanity, "disillusion and regret" (p. 91). So the father taught the son "contemptuous, inflexible negation of all effort" (p. 174).

Immediately after this last passage Conrad revised his manuscript to delete an obvious allusion to Ecclesiastes. *Victory* is Conrad's Baedecker to the Bible, and although he revised the manuscript extensively, he retained all save one of its scriptures, usually intensifying them to increase the volume of his echoes.[3] After commenting on the father's negation, Conrad has Heyst say to himself, " 'And I the son of my father have been caught, too, like the silliest fish of them all' " (p. 174). Then, in the manuscript, Conrad adds, "We are told that all is vanity—but personal vanity seems something that has an existence since it can get hurt in a way that is sensible to the person—to the most superior person."[4] Why did Conrad drop this outright allusion and the observation it provokes when his aim in revising was to intensify Scriptures? Perhaps because the allusion is clumsily done—the Kliszczewski letter without quotation marks. Obviously, though, he could have revised the clumsiness away. Perhaps he deletes it because he does not want to appear to contradict his source, even if to deepen its pessimism, and thereby undermine the authority of the elder

[3] Some of those changes are discussed in chapter 5 below.

[4] *Victory* MS, p. 450, in the Humanities Research Center, University of Texas at Austin.

Heyst as author's voice.[5] Or perhaps he deletes it because the observation it engenders makes little sense. Those two reasons seem plausible. But of a third we can be decently sure: Conrad deletes the heavy allusion to the Preacher because he had just put a subtle one into Heyst's mouth, "'caught, too, like the silliest fish of them all.'" The Preacher illustrates his saying that "time and chance happeneth to them all" with the fate of fishes: "For man also knoweth not his time: as the fishes that are taken in an evil net, and as the birds that are caught in the snare; so are the sons of men snared in an evil time, when it falleth suddenly upon them" (9:11–12). This deletion gives a glimpse into how Conrad composed. Characteristically, Conrad's scriptures come in clusters; evidently thinking of one stimulated thinking of others. This associative method could be dangerous—one scripture following hot upon another, their numbers and density diluting the sense of estrangement Conrad wants to provoke in us. Here, indeed, Conrad risks losing the effect, since Heyst has just taken thought of "'the original Adam'" in him and of how that Adam went about "naming the animals of that paradise he was soon to lose" (pp. 173–74). That is advertisement enough; a third heavy allusion would be too many, and familiarity might breed not contempt but comfort. The subtlety of Heyst's fishes achieves the estranging effect. For the reader with an ear for Scripture will recall Ricardo's words, speaking of Jones, "'I left the sea to follow him'" (p. 125). The manuscript reads clearly "Him."[6] Again, Conrad may have thought that he was going too far, that he could count on his readers

---

[5] A case for the elder Heyst's authority is shrewdly made by William W. Bonney, *Thorns & Arabesques: Contexts for Conrad's Fiction*, pp. 182, 190, 193–94.

[6] *Victory* MS, p. 328.

getting the point without the capital. If Ricardo's words recur as a still small voice for the reader when Heyst thinks of the fish, two antithetical scriptures collide. We become Elijahs outside the cave, astonished to discover that what we had expected was so unlike what came to pass. Scripture is made to estrange us from Scripture.

The deletion, then, is powerful witness to how much the Preacher was on Conrad's mind when he wrote *Victory*. As Elijah found out, a vocal absence can be very convincing. But we shall see that *Victory* outdoes Ecclesiastes, even more blank than the Preacher about the futility of human action in the face of universal vanity.

Ecclesiastes moves Conrad to dark ironies; Job, to comedy. With a perverse delight in playing against his text, Conrad likes to raise a smile when he alludes to the classic tale of misery. No small part of the comedy is that Conrad's allusions to Job poke out incongruously, neither metaphors nor mixed metaphors but parodies.

"Youth" once more gives an example. There Conrad flaunts the famous text, "Yet man is born to trouble, as the sparks fly upward" (Job 5:7). As the crew readies the boats to abandon the aptly named *Judea,* an immense flame spurts up: " 'There were cracks, detonations, and from the cone of flame the sparks flew upward, as man is born to trouble, to leaky ships, and to ships that burn' " (p. 31). Reversing the order of the clauses and adding the two droll prepositional phrases deface the original just enough to make it grotesque. No longer a lesson in patience, Job becomes a type of the universal joke. The joke becomes rather too obvious when young Marlow is welcomed to port by the curses of the captain of another ship aptly named, the *Celestial.* Instead of the Lord answering Job out of the whirlwind,

Marlow gets the captain of the *Celestial* cursing him out of the night, a parody of Job's Lord, raging "'aloud in two languages, and with a sincerity in his fury that almost convinced me that I had sinned against the harmony of the universe'" (p. 39). His universal economy is, of course, God's theme in Job's theophany. But if the joke approaches slapstick, it has some subtle touches. The captain mistakes Marlow's boat for the port authority's, and he rages at Marlow because the jetty light is out. The mistake corrected, the captain asks rhetorically: "'See—there's no light. It's out, isn't it? . . . You can see for yourself it's out—don't you'" (p. 40). Job's familiars will hear the rhetorical question the Lord puts to his victim, "Where is the way where the light dwelleth?" (38:19). Conrad converts Heaven blazing into the head to gaiety—not transfiguring for Marlow, perhaps, but certainly for us.

Just as the blazing *Judea* stimulates a comic rendition of Job, so do the blasted ships Conrad describes in *The Mirror of the Sea*. In a graveyard at the Import and Export basins of the West India Docks, "wicked ships . . . would have full leisure to repent of their sins, sorrowful and naked, with their rent garments of sailcloth stripped off them, and with the dust and ashes of the London atmosphere upon their mast-heads. For the worst of ships would repent if she were given time" (p. 119). Conrad combines two texts, Job before his second affliction, when he "rent his mantle, and shaved his head, and fell down upon the ground . . . [saying], Naked came I out of my mother's womb, and naked shall I return thither," and Job after the Lord's impressive theophany, when Job says, "Wherefore I abhor myself, and repent in dust and ashes" (1:20–21, 42:6). Unlike Job, however, these ships will never be restored to their former estate, damned "into the limbo of things that have served their time" (p. 120). The immense gulf between tenor and vehicle suggests, though, that Scripture, too, has served its time.

Parody also dominates the text Conrad jams into *Nostromo* and *A Personal Record*, another borrowing from the theophany, God's war-horse: "He saith among the trumpets, Ha, ha; and he smelleth the battle afar off, the thunder of the captains, and the shouting" (39:25). In *Nostromo* the allusion is extremely disconcerting, a joke as preface to the narrative of Decoud's suicide. The steamer carrying Barrios, his troops, and Nostromo to the rescue of Sulaco bears down upon Great Isabel. Nostromo sees the lighter's dinghy adrift. He jumps overboard, swims to the boat, and, examining it, finds the brown spot that the reader knows to be the sole visible sign of Decoud's passing. Then we are told that Barrios had never asked Nostromo about Decoud because, "scenting the battle from afar," he "had not wasted his time" (p. 493). With that certain echo heard, we can appreciate what Conrad is about just before Nostromo jumps. We can hear the horse's laugh and the thunder of the captains and the shouting. Nostromo has spotted the dinghy:

"*Por Dios,* I know her. She belongs to my Company." "And, *por Dios,*" guffawed Barrios, in a noisy, good-humoured voice, "you belong to me. I am going to make you a captain of the cavalry directly we get within sight of a horse again."

"I can swim far better than I can ride, mi General," cried Nostromo, pushing through to the rail with a set stare in his eyes. Let me—"

"Let you? What a conceited fellow that is," bantered the General jovially, without even looking at him. "Let him go! Ha! ha! ha! He wants me to admit that we cannot take Sulaco without him! Ha! ha! ha! Would you like to swim off to her, my son?"

A tremendous shout from one end of the ship to the other

42

stopped his guffaw. Nostromo had leaped overboard; and his black head bobbed up far away already from the ship. The General muttered an appalled "*Cielo!* Sinner that I am" in a thunderstruck tone. [P. 491]

Even the innocent piety of the Spanish exclamations acquires a bizarre tonality. Inviting the reader to compare "the one-eyed tiger slayer" with the pawing war-horse of the Lord, emblem of the mysterious magnificence of a creation that man cannot presume to understand, is peculiar rhetoric at this special point in the novel. Conrad could depend on his English readers scenting the famous phrase and perhaps the elaborate joke preceding it. How he imagined his reader would respond, it passeth my understanding to guess. But for this reader the grotesque intrusion affects a startling awareness of the fiction as fiction.[7]

Just before we come to Decoud's suicide, Conrad deliberately shakes the realistic foundation of his work, its appearance as history. Laughter intrudes into the great silence that afflicts Decoud, the laughter of the horse, of the reader, of Conrad. Perhaps we are to imagine Decoud in his isolation, without comforters, another victim of the universal joke for whom no voice speaks out of the whirlwind. Instead of the voice, instead of the cursing captain of the *Celestial,* a laughing author. But why laugh at "the exile of utter unbelief," whose "want of faith" is amply justified by the allusive parody? In the previous chapter, I mentioned Decoud as one of Conrad's inexplicable converts, a Jacob wrestling. But Decoud, we are explicitly told, does not wrestle, for "he was not fit to grapple with himself" (p. 497). Perhaps the estranging laughter of the parody says that Decoud

---

[7] J. Hillis Miller, *Poets of Reality*, p. 18–19, claims that such estrangements are "the aim of all Conrad's fiction."

43

is neither Jacob nor Job. He neither wrestles nor protests. He is not Hirsch. Decoud is a negative convert to the wisdom of the elder Heyst, "'contemptuous, inflexible negation of all effort.'" Decoud finds action unreal, "exertion . . . senseless" when he beholds "the universe as a succession of incomprehensible images" (pp. 497, 498). But beholding the void is not sufficient unto itself; the tale hangs on how one reacts to that perception. The elder Heyst dies peacefully in bed. Hirsch spits at his tormentor. Compared to their responses, Decoud's self-pitying hebetude deserves our dark laughter. He is a comedian.

The laughter of *A Personal Record* is made of much lighter stuff. Conrad unships a pony for his original Almayer. But the little pony objects: "He was fierce, terrible, angry, warlike; he said ha! ha! distinctly, he raged and thumped" (p. 79). The pony is to the horse of the Lord as the plaintive Almayer is to Job, a parody of Scripture. Decoud is the more impressive actor, but he and Almayer take on the same role in the same comedy.

It would be wise to keep in mind that Conrad generally uses Job for comedy when one considers the well-known allusion in *Victory* likening Jones to Job's adversary. When God asks Satan where he has been, the Adversary replies, "From going to and fro in the earth, and from walking up and down in it" (1:7, 2:2). To the same question put by Heyst, Mr. Jones replies that "'he was a rebel now, and was coming and going up and down the earth'" (pp. 317–18). This is one of the scriptures Conrad intensified in his revision. In the manuscript, the passage reads, "'and was coming and going on earth.'"[8] Evidently Conrad checked his memory against the Authorized text, eager that his readers

[8] *Victory* MS, p. 895.

should not miss the point. But what point? Perhaps Conrad's parodic uses of Job should caution us against the usual way of grappling with the inconsistencies of *Victory*, making it a serious allegory. Seymour L. Gross, one of the first readers to detect Job's Satan in Mr. Jones, erects an allegory of love out of the perception, and his lead has been followed by others.[9] For Gross the allusion makes Jones a type of "that demonic principle that has neither name nor identity," a principle that, in the allegory, Lena overcomes. But Gross and his followers are unaware of the history of Conrad's uses of Job and of the glut of scriptural allusions in *Victory* itself, an elaborate series of intrusive gestures that fixes a great gulf between Conrad and his tale. Resorting to allegory, Northrop Frye remarks, "has deposited a large terminal moraine of confusion in modern criticism."[10] Some critics of *Victory* have done their part to glaciate the book. The error arises from failing to distinguish Conrad's mind from the minds of his creatures. It would be accurate to say that Jones likes to think that he is the demonic principle, as Almayer likes to think himself Job. But Jones is no more the Adversary than Barrios is the war-horse of the Lord. The allusion is a parody. We are meant to laugh at Jones,

[9]Seymour L. Gross, "The Devil in Samburan: Jones and Ricardo in *Victory*," *NCF* 16 (June, 1961):81–85. Muriel C. Bradbrook, *Joseph Conrad*, p. 62, seems to have been the first of the allegorists of *Victory*. Others are Kingsley Widmer, "Conrad's Pyrrhic *Victory*," *TCL* 5 (October, 1959):125; and R. W. B. Lewis, "The Current of Conrad's *Victory*," in *Trials of the Word*, p. 151, both of whom endorse but regret the supposed allegory. Those who like it, besides Gross and Bradbrook, include Donald Dike, "The Tempest of Axel Heyst," *NCF* 17 (September, 1962), p. 107; and John A. Palmer, *Joseph Conrad's Fiction: A Study in Literary Growth*, pp. 168–69, 173, 188. A voice crying out against the allegorists is Douglas B. Park, "Conrad's *Victory*: The Anatomy of a Pose," *NCF* 31 (1976):150–69. See also Bonney, *Thorns*, pp. 238–39, n. 54.

[10]Northrop Frye, *Anatomy of Criticism: Four Essays*, p. 90.

not to dignify him with satanic grandeur. We are meant to smile at Lena, too. We shall see how broadly when I turn to the scriptural origins of the title, *Victory.*

Conrad plucks many "dry leaves . . . for a tender memento from the tree of knowledge," as he puts it in *A Personal Record* (p. 110). We examined a few of those mementos in the last chapter. Allusions to the first three chapters of Genesis are so common in Conrad and in English literature generally that they have become dead metaphors, dry indeed, and it requires formidable rhetoric to breathe the breath of life into them. Conrad often succeeds.

One would expect Conrad to like the second verse of Genesis: "And the earth was without form and void; and darkness was upon the face of the deep. And the Spirit of God moved upon the face of the waters." He spent twenty years upon that face and then dedicated his fiction to returning us to the no-time of darkness and the void. Conrad recalls that face early and late in his writing: when Giorgio Viola, a devoted reader of the Bible, observes that "the spirit of liberty is upon the waters" (*Nostromo*, p. 341); when "the unchanged face of the waters" amazes the commanding officer of "The Tale" (p. 63); when, in *The Arrow of Gold*, M. George's infatuation inspires him to the ridiculous conceit that "Rita's own spirit hovered over the troubled waters of Legitimacy" (p. 242); when, regretting the shrunken globe, Conrad in "Geography" says, "For a change had come over the spirit of cartography" (p. 13). The last two samples illustrate Conrad's later preference for parodying Scripture, exploiting it for comedy. Compare those samples with Conrad's uses of the second verse of Genesis in *Heart of Darkness.* "Forthwith a change came over the waters," Conrad writes as prelude to the adventurous genesis of the Thames

46

(p. 46). Then, when Marlow pushes off from the Central Station toward Kurtz, he describes "'travelling in the night of first ages,'" when the earth was without form, when "'The earth seemed unearthly'" (p. 96). The journey to Kurtz is a journey out of history, beyond the backward and abysm of time, before Creation, before God. There Kurtz, in his summing up of this journey, is made to pronounce a Last Judgment in the words from another text from Genesis describing Abram's first experience of theophany: "... an horror of great darkness fell upon him" (15:12).[11] These are metaphors, not parodies. Early Conrad displays a keen perception of the intolerable terror of the Lord: *le néant* of Abram's darkness.

Scripture is normative, too, in "The End of the Tether" and *Lord Jim*, where Conrad uses another commonplace from the Creation, Adam's vow of fidelity, "bone of my bone, and flesh of my flesh" (2:23). Of his daughter, Captain Whalley says to Van Wyk, with perception greater than Whalley knows, "'You can't understand how one feels. Bone of my bone, flesh of my flesh; the very image of my poor wife'" (p. 293). Whalley's dilemma is to be caught between fidelities, fidelity to his profession or to his flesh. He chooses flesh. But faith is the price he pays. Like Giorgio Viola a "patriarch," and like him a devoted reader of the Bible, Whalley too sees himself and his world as if reflected in the dark glass of Scripture. Thus he figures himself another Samson and hopes to shake a temple down (p. 301). Unlike the Garibaldino's, though, Whalley's faith is ortho-

[11] See C. T. Watts, Conrad's "Heart of Darkness": A Critical and Contextual Discussion, p. 12. Discussing the title's sources, Watts cites a passage from Wells's *Time Machine*, its final sentence reading, "A horror of this great darkness came on me." Watts is evidently unaware of Wells's source.

dox. He had prayed "All the days of his life . . . for daily bread, and not to be led into temptation, in a childlike humility of spirit" (p. 325; see also pp. 171, 304). But as his blindness advances, his faith wanes, and he sees universal darkness, and he is no more like a little child. In his extremity he becomes an authentic imitation of Job, praying "for death till the prayers had stuck in his throat"—like Job, one of "the bitter in soul; Which long for death, but it cometh not" (Job 3:20–21; see also 6:8–9). Yet he is denied Job's theophany. Before his suicide he thinks that "God had not listened to his prayers," and Conrad needs biblical imagery to explain why: "The light had finished ebbing out of the world; not a glimmer. It was a dark waste" (p. 333; Matt. 5:14). Whalley's tragedy envelops paradoxes of fidelity. "The End of the Tether" and "Youth" are the poles of Conrad's ambivalence toward the faith of his father. "Youth" turns a childish day to parody, its *Judea* and *Celestial* grotesque symbols of the Old Testament and the New. But to render on tragic terms an old man's loss of his orthodox faith requires of the writer some sympathy with that faith. He must believe that the loss is in fact tragic. This tension between scorn and sympathy for traditional Judeo-Christian conceptions, this active agnosticism, controls Conrad's art until *Under Western Eyes.*

Jim, too, must choose between fidelities. But he does not choose flesh. He takes a shadow, "eternal constancy" not to Adam's Eve but to "a shadowy ideal of conduct" (p. 416). The choice makes Jim less sympathetic, less tragic than Captain Whalley, but more heroic and fascinating. Marlow moots the issue of conflicting fidelities. Reviewing the last letter Jim received from his parsonfather, Marlow muses sardonically, "'. . . bone of his bone, flesh of his flesh,'" (p. 342). The faith of his father creates no conscious predicament for Jim, though it is hard to say what Jim is conscious of. But dramatic irony apparently rules when Jim, bested in his wrestling with Gentleman Brown, swears to his people "'that their welfare was his welfare, their losses his losses, their mourning his mourning'" (p. 392).

Unwitting, Jim mimics Ruth's vow to Naomi: "Intreat me not to leave thee, or to return from following after thee: for whither thou goest, I will go; and where thou lodgest, I will lodge: thy people shall be my people, and thy God my God: Where thou diest, will I die, and there will I be buried: the Lord do so to me, and more also, if ought but death part thee and me" (Ruth 1:16–17). The classic scripture of fidelity speaks against Jim. Ruth's idea of fidelity nourishes a family, a community, and a faith; Jim's fidelity to "'a fixed idea of conduct'" murders Dain Waris, desolates Jewel, and kills himself. Or perhaps we are not to imagine that Jim is innocent of his mimicry, since he is a minister's son. If so, what could better illustrate Jim's incomprehension of his case than his scriptural mixed metaphor?

One last cliché from Genesis. Conrad enjoys God's curse of the serpent: "And I will put enmity between thee and the woman, and between thy seed and her seed; it shall bruise thy head, and thou shall bruise his heel" (3:15). For a modern reader the grammatical confusions of this text are cleared up in the Douay rendering: "She shall crush thy head, and thou shalt lie in wait for her heel." A modern translation, where the plural pronoun stands for "seed," gives "strike at their heel." My point, of course, is that tradition, derived from Romans 16:20, has altered the text, the serpent bruised by rather than bruising Eve's heel. Conrad follows tradition, most famously in *Victory,* when Lena extracts Ricardo's knife, "the venom of the viper in her paradise . . . and the viper's head all but lying under her heel"

(p. 398). Allegorists insist on treating this passage as the author's perception. There is allegory here, but it is in Lena's demented mind, a mind like Jones's shot through with religious delusions. More about this when I come to the entitling "victory." For now, it is enough to remark the history of this text in Conrad. On two other occasions he makes it mirror a deranged personality.

That de Barral is mad no one, perhaps, would question, and we hear him employ Eve's heel to dramatize his plight. Powell overhears de Barral saying to Flora "'something nasty about being "under the heel" of somebody or other,'" and later de Barral says directly to Powell in words that leave no doubt that scripture is on his "lurid" brain: "These conspiracies are the devil. She has been leading me on, till she has fairly put my head under the heel of that jailer, of that scoundrel, of her husband. . . . Treachery! Bringing me low. Lower than herself. In the dirt. That's what it means. Doesn't it? Under his heel!" (pp. 298, 432–33). Then de Barral—or Mr. Smith, as Powell knows him—drinks the poison he had meant for Anthony. Marlow interprets, thinking upon "the sombre and venomous irony in the obsession which had mastered that old man" (p. 435). Like Mr. Jones of *Victory*, Mr. Smith, a lucid symbolic contradiction in his madness, imagines himself the devil hedged about. Quite possibly Conrad saw the kinship between his two serpents: for half of the manuscript of *Victory*, Jones's name is "Mr. Smith."[12] Smith–de Barral's insanity—in which he bears all and bares all—is merely the obverse of Lena's.

A similarly lucid symbolic contradiction peeks out of the mind of another woman dressed in black with a knife, Winnie Verloc's in the splendid scene of wrestling with

[12]Until *Victory* MS, p. 698; cf. *Victory*, p. 260.

Comrade Ossipon. Verloc is dead, and Winnie's imagining of the gallows has plunged her into the waters of "madness and despair" where she will drown. At this stage it has led her to transfigure Comrade Ossipon into her "saviour," her radiant "messenger of life" (pp. 292–99). Winnie clinging to his legs, Comrade Ossipon has the unlucky thought that she "twined round him like a snake." Winnie, still at his feet, gives his venomous thought a voice: " 'Tom, you can't throw me off now. . . . Not unless you crush my head under your heel. I won't leave you' " (p. 291). Winnie's text could not, for her purposes, be more pathetically inapt. For Conrad's, though, it is perfectly apt, an excellent conceit for madness and despair.

That is consistently the symbolic value of Eve's heel in Conrad. To make a serious allegory out of Lena's heel violates the context both of *Victory* and of Conrad's fiction as a whole, turning Conrad's meaning inside out: allegorical imagining is a cause and an effect of madness.

Even a dull soul innocent of Scripture would know the following text. None better illustrates Conrad's genius for diverting the commonplace from its usual channel to irrigate strange fields of thought:

Belshazzar the king made a great feast to a thousand of his lords, and drank wine before the thousand. Belshazzar, whiles he tasted the wine, commanded to bring the golden and silver vessel which his father Nebuchadnezzar had taken out of the temple which was in Jerusalem; that the king, and his princes, his wives, and his concubines, might drink therein. Then they brought the golden vessels that were taken out of the temple of the house of God which was at Jerusalem; and the king, and his princes, his wives, and his concubines, drank in them. They drank wine, and praised the gods of gold, and of silver, of brass, of iron, of wood, and of stone. In the same hour came forth fingers of a man's hand, and wrote over against the candlestick upon the plaister of the wall of the king's palace: and the king saw the part of the hand that wrote. [Dan. 5:1–5]

When his astrologers fail to interpret the hand of God, Belshazzar, at his queen's behest, sends for Daniel. Daniel tells him that God's hand has come because the king profaned the holy vessels. Then Daniel reads the writing on the wall illuminated by the fiery candle:

Then was the part of the hand sent from him; and this writing was written. And this is the writing that was written, MENE, MENE, TEKEL, UPHARSIN. This is the interpretation of the thing: MENE, God hath numbered thy kingdom, and finished it. TEKEL; Thou art weighed in the balances, and art found wanting. PERES; Thy kingdom is divided, and given to the Medes and the Persians. Then commanded Belshazzar, and they clothed Daniel with scarlet, and put a chain of gold about his neck, and made a proclamation concerning him, that he should be the third ruler in the kingdom. In that night was Belshazzar the king of the Chaldeans slain. And Darius the Median took the kingdom, being about threescore and two years old. [Dan. 5:24–31]

From "The End of the Tether" to *The Rescue*, Conrad delights in diverting this familiar tale and changing it utterly. In his last two sentences the apocalyptist states his theme: God is the master of history. Conrad's meaning is not that. Instead of an instance of the sacred entering history, the mysterious characters become a symbol of the void.

Captain Whalley and Charles Gould make the curious error of mistaking the writing on the wall for a sign of good fortune. We are not told whether Gould reads the Bible, but Whalley does, and so his misreading is especially glaring, the only point in the tale where Conrad's irony is unsympathetic. Well before the suicide at his tether's end—weighting himself with bars of iron like Brierly in *Lord Jim*, as Decoud weights himself with bars of silver, for insurance against the imperious call of life—Whalley sees and misreads the writing on the wall. Imagining a proper manner of dying, in fact, trusting "to his Maker to provide a manner of going out of which he need not be ashamed," Whalley gazes "fixedly with a rapt expression, as though he had seen his Creator's favorable decrees written in mysterious characters on the wall" (pp. 291–92). As Whalley's faith wanes, however, he understands his misinterpretations, thinking that "the hand of God was upon him" (p. 303). But Conrad may also have in mind a radical rereading of another Scripture: "'And now, behold, the hand of the Lord is upon thee, and thou shalt be blind'" (Acts 13:11). Paul blinds the sorcerer Elymas because the sorcerer had sought "to turn [a convert] away . . . from the faith," and the blindness is taken as proof of "the doctrine of the Lord." But Whalley's hand of God dealing out blindness is proof that the universe is dark, a "dark waste" without end (pp. 324, 333). Such an insight is denied Charles Gould. "Gazing abstractly," like Whalley, Gould meditates writing a letter to his American partner, Holroyd the Puritan, about his scheme to back a revolution with the wealth of the mine. Gould sees the words "as if written in letters of fire upon the wall" (p. 379). Gould misreads, and Conrad flatters us, allowing us to be Daniels, to foresee that the kingdom of the King of Sulaco will be divided because, like the ancient king, Gould has "praised the gods . . . of silver." In both instances, Conrad's distancing similitudes, "as though" and "as if," signal the irony. Whalley and Gould forget that the writing on the wall for God's correspondents always bodes ill.

Two of Conrad's women, Sophia Antonovna and Edith Travers, are allowed to read the writing on the wall aright. Sophia Antonovna lives up to her name, saying to Razumov: "'Crush the Infamy. A fine watchword! I would . . . hang it out in letters of fire in that empty sky for a sign of hope and terror—a portent of the end'" (p. 263). She renders exactly the biblical context, that the mysterious characters signify terror for the oppressor who receives them, hope for the interpreting oppressed. But that she is such a literalist may not redound to her credit. Sophia of the empty sky is the Paul of revolution. Despite her atheism, Sophia is a typologist, and that contradiction implies Conrad's contempt. Like Paul, she has engaged "'in the good fight'" (p. 260); 1 Tim. 6:12, 2 Tim. 4:7), and like Paul, who refers to Abraham's sojourn "in the land of promise, as in a strange country" (Heb. 11:9), Sophia refers to the journey of her comrade, Yaklovitch, to America as an exile "'in a strange country'" (p. 240). She heartens Razumov as Paul heartens Timothy, like him scorning death (p. 250; 2 Tim. 4:6), like him cautioning against "foolish and unlearned questions" or "'conventional trifles'" that "gender strifes" among the brethren (p. 254; 2 Tim. 2:23). Like Paul, she alludes to Daniel (2 Tim. 4:17). Hers, then, is no real revolution, for she imposes upon her activities a justificatory vision derived from the base of Western culture. Of course, it can be argued that Conrad has no authentic understanding of revolutionists, that Sophia sounds like Paul because Conrad cannot conceive of revolutionists in terms other than those drawn from Western cultural assumptions. But by now it should be abundantly evident that Conrad's scriptural allusions are carefully wrought devices of characterization, and in Sophia's case she is too consistently the Paul of revolution to doubt that Conrad wants to portray her in that highly specific guise. Those are not the only terms available to him. Nonetheless, it may not be Sophia's mind that Conrad characterizes through those allusions. It may be the mind of his narrator, the elderly professor of languages, who cannot conceive of things Russian except he clothe them in imaged phrases from the English Bible.

There is, however, little doubt of Edith Travers's perceptiveness when she reads Tom Lingard's letters of fire. In them she senses his mania, the Yahwistic delusion of that thief in the night. "'What can there be at stake,'" she asks Lingard, who replies according to our source, "'A kingdom.'" Then, as he tries to articulate his scheme to restore those Israelites, Hassim and Immada, to their promised land, to redeem a "subjugated world" like Christ, Mrs. Travers follows his stammerings "as if outlined in words of fire." Instead of "Mene, Mene, Tekel, Upharsin," Lingard stammers, "'Belarab, Daman, Tengaa, Ningrat.'" The words "stood out alone as if written on the night; they took on a symbolic shape; they imposed themselves upon her senses, . . . and these barbarous sounds seemed to possess an exceptional energy, a fatal aspect, the savour of madness" (pp. 261–63). Edith may, and we surely should, see in these barbarous symbols Lingard's divine madness written upon the night. So should we see Sophia Antonovna's and Charles Gould's. Indeed, while Gould reads his writing to himself, combining the roles of God, Belshazzar, and Daniel, his wife thinks that "a man haunted by a fixed idea is insane" (p. 379).

In Conrad's personal symbolism of ordinary scriptures, the writing on the wall, like Eve's heel, savors of delusion or madness, a delusion that consists in refusing to see that the wall is perfectly blank. That final significance of the symbol Conrad interprets for us in *The Secret Agent*, where he wrings the least possible meaning out of this text as Winnie prepares to murder Adolf Verloc, who in his last moments is privileged to see nothing at all.

While Verloc reclines on a sofa, Winnie stares fixedly, like Whalley and Gould, beyond him: "Mr. Verloc glanced over his shoulder. There was nothing behind him: there was just the whitewashed wall. The excellent husband of Winnie Verloc saw no writing on the wall" (p. 240). The image becomes increasingly ominous. Winnie sets "her features into a frozen contemplative immobility addressed to a whitewashed wall with no writing on it" (p. 241). Conrad stresses the absence of writing, the contrast with his source. Daniel's script, however ill-omened for Israel's enemies, would at least relieve the mounting nihilism. But in the ensuing allusions there is not even "no writing," the vacancy squared by itself. Winnie gazes "at the whitewashed wall. A blank wall—perfectly blank," looks "fixedly at a blank wall" (pp. 244, 245).[13] Yet when she mentally assumes "the biblical attitude of mourning—the covered face, the rent garments," and "the sound of wailing and lamentation [fills] her head" (p. 246), Winnie seems our modern Rachel and Stevie Israel's child: "A voice was heard in Ramah, lamentation and bitter weeping; Rachel weeping for her children refused to be comforted for her children, because they were not" (Jer. 31:15; see also Matt. 2:18). But Winnie is not Rachel. The Lord comforts mother Israel, promising that her children "shall come again from the land of the enemy" (Jer. 31:16). The Lord does not speak to Winnie Verloc. God does not write on the wall of the house in Brett Street. Instead, an image of God's intervention in

---

[13]Miller, *Poets of Reality*, p. 63, calls the wall here "a symbol of death," without mentioning the allusion.

history becomes an image of the shadow of death. Instead of writing, Verloc sees too late, not like the ancient king a part of the hand that wrote but "on the wall the moving shadow of an arm with a clenched hand holding a carving knife" (p. 262). In *The Secret Agent* the sacred suffers violent implosions, as in the dreams of that messiah of dynamite, the Professor. Conrad suggests that the "man-made might" of the modern world divorces us from transcendent explanations of history and leaves us defenseless against our own violence. And there was nothing behind Verloc.

This parade of Old Testament commonplaces in Conrad has been brief. I have looked only at those to which Conrad gives specific and personal meaning. I have even ignored one of those, the mark of Cain in "The Secret Sharer" and *Lord Jim,* because I have nothing to subtract from or add to what others have said about it.[14] I have not glossed Marlow's "one of us," the refrain of *Lord Jim,* because I am not persuaded that it is a scriptural allusion.[15] I have ignored

14Louis H. Leiter, "Echo Structures: Conrad's 'The Secret Sharer,'" *TCL* 5 (January, 1960):159–75, mines the Cain allusion. Daniel R. Schwarz, "The Journey to Patusan: The Educations of Jim and Marlow in *Lord Jim,*" *SNNTS*4 (Fall, 1972):454, compares the Cain allusion there to that in "Sharer," while Elliott B. Gose, "Pure Exercises of Imagination: Archetypal Symbolism in *Lord Jim,*" *PMLA* 79 (March, 1964):143–44, remarks that and other echoes biblical.

15Dudley Flamm, "The Ambiguous Nazarene in *Lord Jim,*" *ELT* 11 (1968), refers Marlow's "'one of us'" to Gen. 3:22, and this reading has the sanction of Thomas Moser in his authoritative text of *Lord Jim,* p. 2, n. 2. It appears first in the last sentence of Conrad's Author's Note and in quotation marks. I doubt that he is regressing to the practices of the Kliszczewski correspondence. Marlow uses the phrase ten times, with no hint of a biblical metaphor that I can detect. The phrase appears in other British colonial fictions to designate colonialists of the right sort as distinguished from natives and from whites gone native: "'The long and the short of it is Heaslop's a sahib; he's the type we want, he's other phrases definitely biblical that act as refrains throughout Conrad's work—"delivered into your hands," "in his own image," "by the sweat of his brow"—because they are too many for me and of little metaphoric value except as refrains insisting that readers of Conrad ought to look to their Bibles.

But the performance has been sufficiently varied. The spirit upon the waters, Adam's bone, Eve's heel, Job, the Preacher, and the prophet's lesson in interpretation make a many-colored cast of familiar characters acting out a strange revision of an old play. From this ordinary clay Conrad fashions extraordinary symbols for our time.

---

one of us,' and another civilian who was leaning over the billiard table said, 'Hear, hear!'" E. M. Forster, *A Passage to India*, pp. 25–26. Ronnie Heaslop has the right appearance, "dignified." The first time Marlow uses the phrase, he sounds not unlike Forster's Collector, Turton, at the club: "'I liked his appearance; I knew his appearance; he came from the right place; he was one of us'" (ibid., p. 43). Elsewhere (p. 361), the meaning is pointedly and exclusively racial, a meaning rather at odds with God's in Genesis. Conrad's quotation marks warn us to be on the watch for ironies that tell against Marlow.

POOR MOSES

Until *Under Western Eyes,* we can usually evaluate Conrad's characters, situations, and actions according to the norms implied by scriptural allusions. Whether metaphors or mixed metaphors, the allusions are serious, reliable signs of Conrad's intentions. With *Under Western Eyes,* however, Conrad moves from metaphor to parody, and after it Conrad's allusions are always parodic. This development is quite clear in Conrad's allusions to the history of Israel, especially to Moses and the promised land.

Four of Conrad's nominally nonfictional gestures to the land of promise show the development from metaphor to parody. Early in his writing life (February 2, 1894), Conrad writes to his aunt about her fiction: "And it is very much alive, your little corner of the world, with its silent tumult of passions and its final cry of anguish. The true cry, that—which is only a murmur of the soul that has become exhausted in its struggle towards the Promised Land."[1] It is the "earthy" metaphor of the "little world" of

---

[1] Joseph Conrad, *Letters of Joseph Conrad to Marguerite Poradowska, 1880-1920,* ed. and trans. John A. Gee and Paul J. Sturm, p. 62.

"Books," complete with the paradox of "silent tumult," that Conrad probably founds on the death of Moses (Deut. 34). The irony reacts with, not against, Scripture: Moses' death is an emblem of the human condition. The Lord allows Moses to see the land of promise, then tells him, "but thou shalt not go over thither" (Deut. 34:4). The allusion is imaginative and perfectly orthodox. For Conrad's Polish Catholic aunt the reference could have personal and historical associations, evoking memories of the messianic romanticism of the writer's father, a romanticism partly made in the image of Christ, partly in the image of Israel. A "vision of Poland as the Promised Land" appeared early in the development of Polish romanticism, and the national poet Mickiewicz was addicted to it.[2] Thus Conrad's allusion turns over hallowed ground. Like Moses, nineteenth-century Poles were permitted to view the Promised Land of freedom but prohibited from going thither.

Fourteen years later Conrad again applies the allusion to a writer's work, now Galsworthy's. Galsworthy has given Conrad the manuscript of *Fraternity,* and Conrad reports (August, 1908), "After finishing my reading I sat perfectly still . . . as a pilgrim may sit after a long and breathless ascent, on a commanding summit in view of the promised land."[3] The apparent analogy is that, just as Moses was taken up to the mountain Nebo, Galsworthy takes Conrad to view a fictional world that Conrad can never possess. It would seem a high compliment, very high. Galsworthy is made the Lord of fiction, his art "irresistibly" placing the reader in a "mood . . . of blessed certitude." After such

---

[2] Czesław Miłosz, *The History of Polish Literature*, pp. 163–66, 223–31. See also Hans Kohn, *Pan-Slavism: Its History and Ideology*, 2d ed., rev., pp. 43, 48–49, on Mickiewicz.

[3] G. Jean-Aubry, *Joseph Conrad: Life and Letters*, 2:72.

praise Galsworthy must have been taken aback by Conrad's next letter, a long and rigorous criticism of the breathtaking manuscript.[4] Perhaps Conrad's allusion looks two ways, Galsworthy a Moses, too. Perhaps it looks three ways, the space between tenor and vehicle so outrageously gaping that the integrity of Scripture as a reliable voice of values becomes suspect.

My third specimen comes from the essay "Poland Revisited" (1915). Now the analogy compliments neither side, neither Israel nor Germany. Referring to his trip through Germany to Poland, Conrad writes that he would have preferred

to have fallen asleep on the shores of England and opened my eyes, if it were possible, only on the other side of the Silesian frontier. Yet, in truth, as many others have done, I had "sensed it"—that promised land of steel, of chemical dyes, of method, of efficiency; that race planted in the middle of Europe, assuming in grotesque vanity the attitude of Europeans among effete Asiatics or barbarous niggers; and, with a consciousness of superiority freeing their hands from all moral bonds, anxious to take up, if I may express myself so, the "perfect man's burden."[*Notes*, pp. 146-47]

Now the promised land stands for odious exclusivity, for the hope of "the chosen." Just as Joshua stamped out the natives of Canaan, so Germany purposes to annihilate the "Asiatics" and "niggers," to reenact colonialism on Europe's soil. The justification of the Germanic Tribes is not just analogous to but identical to that of the Tribes of Israel.

After the war Conrad repeats this argument by allusion in "The Crime of Partition" (1919). "The Germanic Tribes," he writes, "had told the whole world . . . what they were

4 Ibid., pp. 76-80.

going to do to the inferior races of the earth, so full of sin and all unworthiness. But with a strange similarity to the prophets of old (who were also great moralists and invokers of might) they seemed to be crying in a desert. Whatever would have been the secret searching of hearts, the Worthless Ones would not take heed" (*Notes,* pp. 124–25). Conrad's irony is vicious, to judge from our own vantage point in modern history. On the one hand, the passage predicts Auschwitz. On the other, it stinks of anti-Semitism. Israel is identical to extirpating Germany. The identity expresses pathological antagonism to the Hebrews of Scripture: it is barbarous to identify Hegel and Nietzsche, Wilhelm and his Prussian officers with the prophet Isaiah crying in the wilderness (Isa. 40:3). Conrad extirpates the validity of Scripture with maddened ferocity that should give us pause about the morality of the later Conrad. He loses control of what, in *The Rescue,* he calls "the sinister irony of allusion" (p. 210). He seems to crave what he condemns. But at least he does not attack the Old Testament merely. He annuls the New Testament, too, an annulment implied in the "'perfect man's burden'" of "Poland Revisited" (see Col. 4:12; 2 Tim. 3:15–17). Here the phrase "so full of sin and all unworthiness" imitates a text that Conrad uses famously in *Heart of Darkness:* ". . . for ye are like unto whited sepulchres, which indeed appear beautiful outward, but are within full of dead men's bones, and of all uncleanness" (Matt. 23:27). At this late date Conrad sees little to choose between Joshua, Jesus, and the German Tribes. And Britain, for that matter, since the "burden" echoes Kipling, too. Conrad is not narrow in his antagonisms.

These extracts illustrate a development in Conrad's fiction, though it is not linear. To *Heart of Darkness,* Conrad's allusions to the history of Israel and the land of promise are reliable metaphors. Parody comes to the surface in *Heart of Darkness,* then submerges until *Under Western Eyes,* a work that is in many respects the critical moment in Conrad's work. That novel's epistemology makes its irony hundred-headed. The intentions of *Victory* and *The Rescue* are much easier to apprehend. Probably the best name for them is not novel or romance but parody: Scripture and all traditional structures and values are annihilated in those later works, sometimes with the same moral implications of "The Crime of Partition." The sinister irony goes as far leftward as it can possibly be pushed.

Conrad's first novel begins with a biblical allusion, once removed, in the epigraph taken from Amiel's *Journal intime* that invites us to see Kaspar Almayer's life and death mirrored darkly in Scripture: "Pauvre Moïse! tu vis aussi onduler dans le lointain les coteaux ravissants de la terre promise, et tu dus étendre tes os fatigués dans une fosse creusée au desert!—Lequel de nous n'a sa terre promise, son jour d'extase et sa fin en exile?"[5] Hence I suggested that the allusion in the Poradowska and Galsworthy letters is probably to Deuteronomy 34. Amiel's question makes Moses stand for all of us. But Kaspar Almayer's end is worse. The Lord at least gives Moses a glimpse of the land he had struggled to attain. In *Almayer's Folly,* however, one man's vineyard is another's wilderness. Sambir is to Tom Lingard "that land of plenty," "the promised land" (p. 8); Almayer yearns to escape Sambir for "Amsterdam, that earthly paradise of his dreams," "the paradise of Europe" (pp. 10, 63). Canaan would not be sufficient for his dreams. Almayer

[5]Henri-Frédéric Amiel, *Fragments d'un journal intime,* 10th ed., 1:50. Conrad omits the first sentence.

would burst past the angels with the flaming swords. Lingard ends exiled in Almayer's paradise, Almayer in Lingard's promised land. The novel closes as it began. Opium-drugged, Almayer stretches out his bones in the abode of his folly that Jim-Eng rechristens "House of heavenly delight" (p. 205). Just as the young Marlow in "Youth" dreams of the East "living and unchanged, full of danger and promise" (p. 41) and journeys to it on the ship *Judea* only to be greeted by the cursing captain of the ship *Celestial,* so Almayer finds the only paradise to be had in a fallen world.

"The Return" (1898) almost realizes Almayer's dream, putting him in London transformed into the wealthy Alvan Hervey, the slight similarity in their names perhaps a sign that Conrad approved the likeness. But the urban wilderness proves no better than Sambir. Hervey's wife is, in his strange imagination, Eve. After reading her farewell—she has intended to run off with a fat poet, only to find the pressures of caste and class too great—Hervey feels "very sick—physically sick—as though he had bitten through something nauseous" (p. 128). Hervey "stood alone, naked and afraid, like the first man on the first day of evil" (p. 134). Like Almayer, Hervey has been living in an opium world, "an extremely charming sphere . . . where nothing is realized and where all joys and sorrows are cautiously toned down into pleasures and annoyances" (pp. 120–21). But unlike Almayer, Hervey discovers that the promised land is an opiate, a metaphor for illusions cultivated so as to make life bearable, one of those illusions being romantic dreams of fulfillment through marital love. Thinking about what course is now open to him, Hervey perceives it to be "the painful explaining away of faults, the feverish raking up of illusions, the cultivation of a fresh crop of lies in the sweat of one's brow, to sustain life, to make it supportable, to make it fair, so as to hand intact to another generation of blind wanderers the charming legend of a heartless country, of a promised land, all flowers and blessings" (p. 134).

But Hervey's brief insight cannot quench the bright and blinding flame of his illusions, in particular the illusion that he is a splendid, deserving, and upright person. When his wife returns without meeting her lover, Hervey figures himself a Levite of society, "the high priest of that temple, the severe guardian of formulas, of rites, of the pure ceremonial" (pp. 155-56). The social code, as he instructs his wife into its mysteries, is coequal to the Law of Moses: "'Nothing that outrages the received beliefs can be right. . . . They are the received beliefs because they are the best, the noblest, the only possible" (p. 157). Hervey's Levite pose and his biblical analogies are meant to show what Conrad calls, in letters to Garnett, "the fabulous untruth of that man's convictions," "the gospel of the beastly bourgeois."[6] Here, then, Scripture is mixed metaphor, but only at Hervey's expense. Out of his own mouth he condemns himself. This is a mind that can twist the simple homily to read, "Deception should begin at home" (p. 170). Conrad's comments to Garnett suggest that he was quite clear in his mind about how and why Alvan Hervey mimes the Bible.

The rhetoric of scripture in *Heart of Darkness* is more ambiguous. *Heart of Darkness* echoes many epic treks, the Exodus among them. Marlow's enforced stay of three months at the Central Station, his interviews with the manager and the manager's secretary (a foretaste of Jones and his "secretary," Ricardo, including the homosexual hint), the "pil-

[6]Joseph Conrad, *Letters from Joseph Conrad, 1895-1924*, ed. Edward Garnett, pp. 107, 111; see also p. 129,

grims" with their "staves," and the various afflictions visited upon them all are reminders of Moses asking Pharaoh to let the children of Israel "journey into the wilderness, and sacrifice to the Lord our God" (Exod. 9:27). Marlow's insistent use of "wilderness," his unnatural comparison of the river to a "desert" (p. 93), and his eventual meeting with a "pitiful Jupiter" (p. 134), whose staked heads, "food for thought," indicate that he had found sacrifices acceptable in his sight (p. 130) are other parts of the fantastic metaphor.

The first bizarre incident at the Central Station recalls two Pentateuchal theophanies. A "grass shed" bursts into flames "so suddenly that you would have thought the earth had opened to let an avenging fire consume all that trash" (p. 76). Moses first sees God, of course, as the burning bush that "burned with fire, and the bush was not consumed" (Exod. 3:2), but Marlow's grass shed is quickly reduced to "a heap of embers." Nor does Marlow hear the voice of God. Instead he hears the "beaten nigger" blamed for the fire "screeching most horribly." The combination of earthquake and fire also recalls the prime reference, the Lord's impressive punishment of Korah and his people for presuming to priestly status. Conrad's language is quite close to that of the Authorized version:

And the earth opened her mouth, and swallowed them up, and their houses, and all the men that appertained unto Korah, and all their goods. . . . And all Israel that were round about them fled at the cry of them: for they said, Lest the earth swallow us up also. And there came out a fire from the Lord, and consumed the two hundred and fifty men that offered incense. [Num. 16: 32–35]

One of the pilgrims, the "indefatigable man" with a hole in his bucket, takes Moses' part, speaking to the people before Korah is consumed. He says of the beaten black: "'Transgression, punishment—bang! Pitiless, pitiless, That's the only way. This will prevent all conflagrations for the future'" (p. 80). It does not for the children of Israel. Furthermore, his words and the beating of the native recall the scapegoat ceremony:

> And Aaron shall lay both his hands upon the head of the live goat, and confess over him all the iniquities of the children of Israel, and all their transgressions in all their sins, putting them upon the head of the goat, and shall send him away by the hand of a fit man into the wilderness: And the goat shall bear upon him all their iniquities unto a land not inhabited: and he shall let go the goat in the wilderness. [Lev. 16:21-22]

Doubting that the black is to blame, Marlow reports that, after this "'brute'" recovered, "he arose and went out—and the wilderness without a sound took him into its bosom again" (pp. 76-77). The compound verb is a biblical signature, a transitional formula used thirty-one times by my count in the Old Testament. Two instances quite close to Conrad's are to be found in 1 Samuel: "And David arose, and went down to the wilderness of Paran"; "Then Saul arose, and went down to the wilderness of Ziph" (25:1, 26:2). The prose of King James's scholars is Marlow's, incessantly intimating that his tale is to the Old Testament as the shadows on the wall of Plato's cave are to reality. *Heart of Darkness* owes some of its power to Conrad's cunning displacement of familiar biblical rhythms and images.

Marlow's remarks about the blaze and the beaten black frame his interview with the manager's secretary. The man acts as secretary because he cannot perform his original assignment, "the making of bricks." "It seems," says Marlow, "he could not make bricks without something—straw maybe," and Marlow opines that the young man may be waiting for "an act of special creation" (p. 77). Marlow self-consciously alludes to Pharaoh's response to Moses' first request, dictating that the Hebrews should "no more [be given] straw to make brick," yet their daily quota remain the same (Exod. 5). So the young man waits for a special creation, for a repetition of the manna and the quails that the Lord provides for his wandering children. The counterpoint of the black's screeches and groans indicates that the metaphor is hopelessly mixed.

Marlow is spared the full tale of plagues. He gets but "five . . . installments" of the Eldorado Exploring Expedition, "an invasion, an affliction, a visitation" (p. 87). The penultimate plague, however, is always with him, "impenetrable darkness," the "beastly, beastly dark" (pp. 114, 149, 150). Surely one of the Scriptures Conrad has in mind throughout is the plague, "darkness over the land of Egypt, even darkness which may be felt," "a thick darkness" (Exod. 10:21–22). That potent image takes specific form in the fog that descends as Marlow draws near the Inner Station, "more blinding than night," "something solid," making "our eyes . . . of no more use to us than if we had been buried miles deep in a heap of cotton-wool. It felt like it, too—choking, warm, stifling" (pp. 101, 197). In *Heart of Darkness,* as in Exodus, the darkness symbolizes moral nullity. Pharaoh is blind to the will of the Lord, the colonizers blind to the religious hypocrisy used to make palatable the brutalizing of a people, "'weaning those ignorant millions of their horrid ways'" (p. 59). During the fire Marlow hears someone say to a gathering of natives, "'Heap of muffs—go to'" (p. 80). The colonizers are indeed "buried miles deep in a heap of cotton-wool," morally entombed by the energetic weaning exemplified in the beating of the black. The metaphor of darkness is not mixed.

The last plague is Kurtz, death. But the end of his earthly remains takes us back again to Amiel and thus indirectly to Moses. Amiel's Moses stretches out his tired bones "dans une fosse creusée." Marlow's "muddy hole" (p. 150) is a fair translation.

The scriptures of *Heart of Darkness* are pure and mixed metaphors violently yoked together. God is a grass shed and a beaten black. The bewitched pilgrims are Egyptian task-masters. The blacks are the Hebrews enslaved, but so are the bewitched pilgrims. Marlow plays Moses to the dilatory pharaonic manager and an Egyptian smitten by the ninth plague. And Kurtz is an enslaving Pharaoh, the Lord, a Hebrew whose people will not let him go, and Moses dead. We can revise Marlow's line to say that everyone in Exodus contributes to the making of Kurtz. The metaphor itself becomes like Kurtz, "weirdly voracious" (p. 134), swallowing up the reader. The discontinuity is especially powerful because in such marked opposition to the rigid continuity of its original. The writers of Exodus mark off the increasingly ferocious plagues one by one, preceding and ending each with set scenes and verbal formulas. The rigidity is extreme and appropriate to the writers' commitments to the glory of the Lord and to a linear conception of history. Conrad's commitments are not those of the writers of Exodus. The analogue is not sequentially developed, as Mann and Joyce develop scriptural analogues. It is erratic, omnivorous. If Conrad "fails to create coherent metaphorical structures,"[7] it is because he has no desire to do so. *Heart of Darkness* argues that the values forming such structures have been so thoroughly degraded into ethical monstrosity that those structures are no longer available.

[7] James Guetti, *The Limits of Metaphor*, p. 1.

Heart of Darkness does not yet annul Scripture, however. The Exodus provides some of the norms by which we can plumb the horror. Moses is not yet the chief of a Germanic tribe. He is not Kurtz. One could even argue that there is no discontinuity in making a beaten black into the Lord. The allusions to Exodus plot how far we have wandered from Horeb. Nonetheless, the concatenation of pure and mixed metaphors in *Heart of Darkness* makes the valuative status of the sacred text equivocal, distinctions of all sorts constantly on the verge of dissolution.

That is not the case in *Nostromo,* where Conrad's allusions to the history of Israel tend to be conservative. Even with very mixed metaphors, we can readily accommodate the distinction between tenor and vehicle. For example, the exodus from Egypt is rehearsed when the people of Sulaco, the wealthy and their servants, flee the city in fear of the Monterists. They seek safety in the wilderness, "the gloom of the Los Hatos woods," with that pious bandit, Hernández, now a general (p. 354). Decoud, in his letter to his sister, writes of preparing the way "for the exodus of the ladies and children" (p. 224). Later the narrator appropriates Decoud's image:

Meantime the exodus had begun. Carretas full of ladies and children rolled swaying across the Plaza, with men walking or riding by their side; mounted parties followed on mules and horses; the poorest were setting out on foot, men and women carrying bundles, clasping babies in their arms, leading old people, dragging along the bigger children. [P. 355]

An image for our time. Conrad seems to have Exodus in mind, though, when "the people took their dough before it was leavened, their kneadingtroughs bound up in their clothes upon their shoulders. . . . about six hundred thousand on foot, that were men, beside children. And a mixed multitude went up also with them; and flocks and herds, even very much cattle" (Exod. 12:34–38). As Moses "took the bones of Joseph with him" (13:19), Antonia takes her dying father, the political patriarch of the people, almost a corpse, "perfectly lifeless" (p. 356). Conrad echoes Conrad when another grass shed catches fire, and descriptions of the blaze punctuate the account of this exodus (pp. 359–61). But like Marlow's, this fire becomes "nothing but a heap of embers" (p. 361). This exodus is not the Exodus.

A similar discrepancy makes itself felt in a verbal allusion that we have seen before. Mrs. Gould, appalled by Holroyd and his partners, asks her husband whether such men can "'really wish to become, for an immense consideration, drawers of water and hewers of wood to all the countries and nations of the earth'" (p. 71). Mrs. Gould perceives that the plutocrats of this earth are more likely to exterminate than to serve. The Holroyds are not Gibeonites (Josh. 9). The true Gibeonites of Costaguana are the Chulos, the Indians of the mine made to draw silver whom no ruse can save. One should not be overtender about Emilia Gould. She perceives the mote in Holroyd's eye and fails to see her own.

What promised land can be built upon materialism? The "business circles" of Costaguana look upon "the Occidental Province as the promised land of safety," a vision made even more grotesque in the rapacious image of Pedrito Montero, for whom Sulaco is "the chosen land of material progress" (pp. 166, 388). The ethical monstrosity that stalks Costaguana is perfectly summed up in General Barrios's naïve, exuberant distortion of Scripture: "We shall convert our swords into ploughshares and grow rich" (p. 148). The prophet writes that, on that remote occasion, we would then "walk in the light of the Lord" (Isa. 2:4-5). But everyone in *Nostromo* serves the gods of silver.

Conrad is no advocate of the prophet's way—not as a rule, at any rate. Of *Nostromo,* E. M. W. Tillyard has cautiously remarked that "Christian thought is behind Conrad's conception of human destiny."[8] How far "behind" it is impossible to say, and "Christian thought" is not a particularly precise formula. But insofar as the rhetorical status of Scripture indicates values, Conrad would seem to be in *Nostromo* far more orthodox than he is in *Heart of Darkness,* far more willing to give authoritative ethical status to Scripture. His arguments against materialism are in no way conspicuously different from those of the prophets and the evangelists. As we shall see in the next chapter, the Sermon on the Mount is the relevant text for *Nostromo* and for *The Secret Agent.* In both, the rhetoric of Conrad's scriptures suggests that he has moved well to the right of the path set from *Almayer's Folly* through *Heart of Darkness.* But with *Under Western Eyes,* he turns leftward again, and he never looks back.

Conrad's elderly professor of languages conceives a pathological hatred for Madame de S——, the grandest feminine light of the Russians in Geneva. Every detail the professor enumerates is acidic: she is a grotesquely painted "witch," the abuser of Tekla, nearly the inmate of a madhouse, a "grinning skull," possibly a double agent (pp. 162-63, 214-

[8]E. M. W. Tillyard, *The Epic Strain in the English Novel*, p. 150. Eloise Knapp Hay, *The Political Novels of Joseph Conrad*, p. 193, remarks in her discussion of *Nostromo* that Conrad's "religious skepticism goes little deeper than the impasse many reach when finding that the presumptions and commitments necessary to maintaining an active faith, especially in respect to men outside the faith, are odious." *Nostromo* supports her, but not most of Conrad's other work.

15). Thus through his venom she acquires the rare distinction of being the least ambiguous of the novel's large cast of characters. In fact, she is not ambiguous at all. Even de P—— is depicted in terms far more varied. Even very minor characters, like Laspara's daughter with a doll, arouse a more complex response. The professor's loathing has the paradoxical effect of making the woman stand out, a cabbage in a bed of herbaceous perennials. For all his claims to restraint, he does not hug his hatred to him, freely admitting, "I had a positive abhorrence for the painted, bedizened, dead-faced, glassy-eyed Egeria of Peter Ivanovitch" (p. 161). That adjectival excess should call into question the narrator's credentials as our historian, if it does not make us question his mental competence altogether. Why abhorrence? Perhaps because Madame de S—— embodies the utter corruption unto death of the traditional values to which the Englishman of many languages so tenaciously clings, in particular the values he invests in the English Bible. "A traveller in a strange country" he calls himself (p. 169), using a scripture to define his urgently equivocal position in Genevan Russia. By a circuitous route —always the only route open—we arrive at the Promised Land. The professor has in mind Paul's Epistle to the Hebrews, where Paul refers to Abraham's sojourn "in the land of promise, as in a strange country" (11:9). The professor's sense of what he is depends upon his sense of the sacredness of the English Bible, a pathetically naïve notion that reveals just how fragile is his sense of an identity. Because Madame de S—— imperils this alien's strange sense of self, he hates her utterly. She debases his promised land of Scripture. And the manner of her doing provides a stunning example of Conrad's brilliant disposition of Scripture in *Under Western Eyes.*

At the close of Razumov's tea party with Madame de S—— and Peter Ivanovitch, the woman finally vents her "murderous hate" for the grand ducal family that, so her tale runs, took her fortune. She envisions that family's extirpation in the bloodbath to come: "Her carmine lips vaticinated with an extraordinary rapidity. The liberating spirit would use arms before which rivers would part like Jordan, and ramparts fall down like the walls of Jericho. The deliverance from bondage would be affected by plagues and by signs, by wonders and by war" (p. 223). The distinctive verb "vaticinated" recalls the professor's indictment of Russian "cynicism," revealed in "the mystic vaticinations of prophets . . . [that make] the Christian virtues themselves appear actually indecent" (p. 67). Madame de S—— makes Scripture indecent for the sake of money and revenge—the dry Jordan, Jericho, and the Lord's "signs" and "wonders in the land of Egypt" (Josh. 3:17, 6:20; Exod. 7:3) signs of her right to property. She actually perverts the professor's promised land and the "Christian virtues" derived from it, the very basis of the stranger's tenuous identity.

Victor Haldin also lays waste to the promised land, and this resemblance to Madame de S—— tells against him. Trying to convert Razumov and to excuse an act that killed not only his intended victim but also his accomplice and some of the peasants he meant to save, Haldin imagines himself Moses and Isaiah's suffering servant. "'You have enough heart,'" he preaches to Razumov, "'to have heard the sound of weeping and gnashing of teeth [de P——] raised in the land. . . . He was uprooting the tender plant. . . . Three more years of his work would have put us back fifty years into bondage—and look at all the lives wasted, all the souls lost in that time'" (p. 16). Since Moses began his mission with a murder, fleeing Egypt for fear of betrayal, the reference to the bondage is not inapt. The up-rooted "'tender plant'" comes from Isaiah's prophecy that the suffering servant, who will deliver Israel from the Babylonian captivity and restore it to the promised land, "shall grow up before the Lord as a tender plant, and as a root out of dry ground" (53:1-2). Haldin matches and mismatches the prophecy. Isaiah says that, before his accusers, the servant "openeth not his mouth" (53:7), just as Haldin refuses to say a word at his interrogation. But the suffering servant earns righteousness "because he had done no violence" (53:9). Haldin is the murdering servant, his vision of his kingship as absurd as the vaticinations of Madame de S——. His sermon to Razumov uncovers his messianic delusions.

But his sermon is far more effective than he knows. Walking back from Ziemianitch's vile stable after beating the drunkard, Razumov is converted to faith in the messianic deliverer to come. Although he recognizes the specific nature of Haldin's disease, "a contagious pestilence" (p. 36), he catches the contagion. Razumov feels "the touch of grace upon his forehead," and he believes that only Isaiah's plant can be Russia's salvation, "the perfect plant" springing "out of the dark soil" (p. 34). Giving Haldin back text for text, now Razumov believes in "the man who would come at the appointed time," in "the great autocrat of the future" (pp. 34, 35). Haldin uses Scripture to justify a slaughter; Razumov uses Scripture to justify giving Haldin up. Like Haldin, Razumov perverts the text: Jeremiah's "chosen man" to come when the Lord "will appoint me the time" (Jer. 49:19, 50:44) is made into a parody as weird as those that fester in Madame de S——'s imagination, into "the great autocrat." So Razumov turns Haldin's typological fantasy against him.

But the source of the fantasy is our narrator, the elderly professor. After all, these are his metaphors, not Haldin's or Razumov's. He insists that he has only translated Razumov's record (pp. 24, 86, 192), but he translates it into the phrases, rhythms, and values of the English Bible. If Sophia Antonovna is the Paul of revolution, if Haldin is the suffering servant, if Razumov is a believer in the chosen man, it is because the professor has made them so. This "traveller in a strange country" settles the land with images he can understand, the English Bible his Baedecker. Often his own images—those not attributed to one of his subjects—clash resoundingly, and in such clashes Conrad intimates that we cannot accept his history uncritically. For example, he sees Mrs. Haldin as both an Egyptian and a Hebrew. When he remarks "the cruel atrocity of Death passing over her head to strike at that young and precious heart" (p. 116), Mrs. Haldin becomes an Egyptian mother, her child taken by the tenth plague (Exod. 12:23). She is the victim of the Passover. Later she becomes mother Israel. The professor applies a text to her that we have seen in *The Secret Agent.* Mrs. Haldin's grief was "more than Rachel's inconsolable mourning" (p. 339)—"Rachel weeping for her children refused to be comforted for her children, because they were not" (Jer. 31:15). Mrs. Haldin's grief surpasses Rachel's because whereas the Lord promises the mothers of Israel "hope in thine end," that their children "shall come again from the land of the enemy" (Jer. 31:16), the Lord does not speak to Mrs. Haldin, and her son will not come again. But the professor's metaphors clash so loudly that they verge on parody. The professor finds things Russian, Natalia's "*mouvements d'âme,*" "inconceivable" (p. 106), so he imposes upon them the literary and cultural tradition of the English Bible in such a bizarre fashion that he imperils the very virtues and values that he prizes. Through his professor, Conrad shows the futility of typological imagining and thus, perhaps, the futility of the sacred text itself as a means of comprehending the modern world.

The epistemology of *Under Western Eyes* is complicated, and I will have more to say about it. Lop off one of its ironies, another springs up. But if the validity of Scripture is only problematic in *Under Western Eyes*, it is not in *Victory* and *The Rescue*. In those late novels, scriptural allusion is pure parody. Allusions to Israel's history furnish several outrageous examples.

Desperate to rid himself of the weird trio that has descended upon his hotel and desperate to revenge himself upon Axel Heyst, the genial Schomberg urges Ricardo to make for Samburan's fabled plunder. Ricardo wants a sign to steer by. Schomberg provides Heyst's neighborly volcano: "'What do you think of a pillar of smoke by day and a loom of fire at night?'" (p. 168). As other readers of *Victory* and Exodus have noted, Schomberg converts the volcano into the Lord leading the Israelites out of Egypt and through the wilderness to the promised land, "before them by day in a pillar of cloud, to lead them the way; and by night in a pillar of fire, to give them light" (Exod. 13:21).[9] But as *Victory* slouches to an end, the volcano has been reduced to "a feather of smoke by day and a cigar-glow at night" (p. 356), the Lord diminished to a cheroot.

The Rescue flogs this theophany mercilessly. When Lingard steers up to the preposterously named Isle of Refuge to remove the Traverses' yacht, preposterously named the

---

[9] Wilfred P. Dowden, *Joseph Conrad: The Imaged Style*, pp. 156–66, notes many biblical allusions in *Victory*, one being the pillar. It has also been remarked by R. W. B. Lewis, "The Current of Conrad's *Victory*," in *Trials of the Word*, p. 157.

Hermit, the Lord guides him even as Ricardo is guided to the island of Samburan: "An invisible fire belched out steadily the black and heavy convolutions of thick smoke, which stood out high, like a twisted and shivering pillar" (p. 57). Then the "black pillar" drifts away "like a threatening and lonely cloud," as the Lord departs from the stiff-necked Israelites. *The Rescue* begins with the reduction that *Victory* develops. Conrad jams together Exodus and Wordsworth. But Lingard sees neither the Lord nor a host of daffodils.[10] Later Edith Travers sees Schomberg's version, a "loom of fire . . . changed into a pillar of smoke" at daybreak (p. 367). Finally the cloud of the Lord appears in a fiercely mocking theophany when the *Emma*—"immense protection," the feminine "Emmanuel"—blows sky-high out of a horrified world, and with it the Hebrews, Hassim and Immada, whom Lingard had promised to lead back in triumph to their land: "A great smoky cloud hung solid and unstirring" (p. 442).

In case we miss the point in *Victory* and *The Rescue,* Conrad flogs another theophany from the saga of Moses. When Moses asks the Lord of the burning bush who he is, the Lord replies that he is the absolutely unconditioned being, free of time and history: "I AM THAT I AM" (Exod. 3:14). The root of Lingard's "infinite illusions" is that he is that unconditioned being. Lingard commands the *Lightning.* Anything else one might say about *The Rescue* is a footnote to that illusory fact. Recalling for Edith his initial

[10] Scripture is not the only victim of Conrad's parody in *The Rescue.* The book bubbles with literary jokes. Consider the faithful messenger, Jaffir, appearing on the Grecian urn, "his firm limbs gleaming like limbs of imperishable bronze through the mass of green leaves that are forever born and forever dying" (pp. 372–73). Conrad reverses the imagery of Keats's third stanza.

quarrel with Travers aboard the *Hermit,* Lingard says, "'It took me all my time to keep my temper down lest it should burn you all up.'" Korah again (see also Num. 11:1–3; Deut. 4:24). Then Lingard defines himself as the Lord of the burning bush: "'I am what I am'" (p. 323). We do not need capitals. Nor do we in *Victory.* Twice Heyst mentions Jones's "'cryptic'" definition, first rendering it "'I am he who is,'" and then in a phrase slightly more like the Lord's, "'I am he that is'" (pp. 317, 376). Although Jones's tautology is somtimes mistaken for another piece of Satanism by those who would squeeze a consistent allegory out of *Victory,* there is no scriptural warrant for that, and R. W. B. Lewis long ago cited the burning bush as the source.[11] The manuscript of *Victory* is again instructive. There, for the first phrasing, Conrad clearly supplies some of the capitals, "'I am He who Is.'"[12] Perhaps he should have kept them; misreadings of *Victory* might have been avoided. For recognizing that Jones dizzily identifies himself with both the Satan of Job and the Lord of the theophany would surely give pause to the most relentless allegorist bent upon creating a serious vision of the insane gambler as the demonic principle stalking through the world, seeking whom he may devour. That is the mistake Lena makes.

If *Victory* has suffered from too much attention of the wrong sort from both realists and allegorists, *The Rescue* has suffered from neglect. William Bonney's recent study is by far the most rigorous and perceptive analysis *The Rescue* has seen. Bonney treats *The Rescue* as an antiromance, a parody, and taking this approach yields him a heavy crop

[11] Lewis, *Trials of the Word,* p. 157.
[12] *Victory* MS, p. 892, in the Humanities Research Center, University of Texas at Austin.

from that fallow ground.[13] For *The Rescue* hacks romance at its root, the Bible, and especially the great teleological romance of the story of Moses.

Moses is ubiquitous in *The Rescue*. He is Belarab, Edith Travers, and a Jewish peddler. The first two metamorphoses are comic wonders. The last has the unpleasant odor of "The Crime of Partition."

Belarab rules the Land of Refuge, possibly an imitation of the Pentateuchal "cities for refuge" (e.g., Num. 35:6). Like Moses, Belarab has led a stiff-necked people into a wilderness (p. 112). Just as things fall apart for the children of Israel when Moses disappears into the mountain to hear the Lord's long monologue, Lingard's project unravels and Belarab's people are thrown into confusion when Belarab disappears into the forest "to indulge for a time in a scrupulous performance of religious exercises" (p. 280). Whether for forty days and nights we are not told.

Moses is Edith Travers, Moses come down from the mountain with a shining face. To spare his people the unbearable brilliance, Moses assumes a veil when he converses with them (Exod. 34:29–35). Edith has a "radiant face," a "complexion so dazzling in the shade that it seemed to throw out a halo round her head" (p. 139). When she throws off her accustomed hood, her face is "fiercely lighted," and even with it on "an intense and unearthly white" (pp. 214, 236). Her eyes shine "'like rays of light'" (p. 242). When we first come upon Edith, she speaks "from behind the veil of an immense indifference" (p. 125), and as the action draws toward the bang of the *Emma,* we are incessantly reminded of whether Edith is veiled or unveiled. Aboard

[13]William W. Bonney, *Thorns & Arabesques: Contexts for Conrad's Fiction,* pp. 125–48. Bonney notes several biblical allusions, as well as allusions to Shelley, Spenser, and Homer.

the *Emma* she appears to Jorgenson "with a boldly un-veiled face" (p. 366), at which apt moment she sees "the loom of fire [change] into a pillar of smoke" (p. 367). She reverses Moses, deliberately assuming her "'face veil,'" her scarf, when in the stockade with Lingard, for, she says, "'nothing will persuade me that there isn't some change in my face'" (p. 399; see also pp. 402, 404, 436). Edith herself bids the reader beware. Yanked into the stockade—birth imagery reversed (p. 394), James Wait backwards—Edith loses a sandal and her scarf. She is frantic to find the sandal because a "lost sandal was as symbolic as a dropped veil" (p. 396), symbolic of Lingard's lordship, which Edith denies. Before the Lord, Moses removes his shoes and his veil. Edith is Moses in a mirror.

The fun-house mirror of Conrad's later works some-times reflects grotesques that in turn reflect an embittered strain in Conrad's imagination. *Victory* is a gallery of dis-torting mirrors. *The Rescue* is more restrained, its parodies of Moses and the Lord generally well-behaved annulments by laughter, and thus very effective. But once Conrad loses his restraint, in the nasty little scene with the Jewish peddler.

Jorgenson is among a group of traders, one "a man with hooked features and of German extraction who was sup-posed to be agent for a Dutch crockery house—the famous 'Sphinx' mark." The traders discuss the change in Lingard, "King Tom," and the one with hooked features exclaims that Lingard is simply mad, "'matt, matt as a Marsh Hase,'" because Lingard had threatened to "'shuck [him] oferboard'" when he came to peddle his "'first class grockery.'" Laugh-ing, one of the men replies, "'Why, Mosey, there isn't a mangy cannibal left in the whole of New Guinea that hasn't got a cup and saucer of your providing.'" But Jorgenson has another explanation: "'you're a Dutch spy.'" At this the "'agent of the Sphinx mark'" leaps up furious, curses the "'Vordamte English pedlars,'" and storms out. "'Why don't you let daylight into him?'" an American gun seller asks. "'Oh, we can't do that here,'" says another, and the American replies, "'you law-abiding, get-a-summons, act-of-parliament lot of sons of Belial—can't you?'" (pp. 95–96). But the "sons of Belial" were in fact practicers of "abomination," heretics, and the scene reenacts Moses' curse upon them (Deut. 13:13–18). They are the agents of the Sphinx mark, urging the children of Israel to "serve other gods," and the city they contaminate must be utterly destroyed. Conrad reduces Moses to "mosey," a hooked parody who served Egyptians.[14] The caricature sneers.

Although this scene is not representative of Conrad's scriptural rhetoric in *The Rescue,* it exemplifies the wholly negative strategy of *Victory* and *The Rescue.* Both works are so nihilistic that they reject the validity of traditional structures. They are not novels. They are not allegories. Character, setting, and action exist solely to put flesh on parody. Frye calls parody "a technique of disintegration."[15] That is Conrad's technique in these late works, a radical obliteration of traditional structures and their values. Mr. Vladimir of *The Secret Agent* would like to throw a bomb into pure mathematics, but he settles for science. In *Victory* and *The Rescue,* Conrad hurls the bomb, but into the English Bible.

[14] Adam Gillon, "The Merchant of Esmeralda—Conrad's Archetypal Jew," *PolR* 9 (Autumn, 1964):3–20, is mistaken when he claims that Hirsch in *Nostromo* and Yankel in "Prince Roman" are the only Jews in Conrad. Besides Mosey, Julius Laspara in *Under Western Eyes* is another. Gillon, however, is probably correct in his evaluation of Conrad's anti-Semitism, that Conrad shared "the general attitudes and prejudices of his age" (ibid., p. 14). I also agree that Conrad transforms Hirsch into a figure of dignity. The later Mosey is indicative of a sad change in Conrad's imagination.

[15] Northrop Frye, *Anatomy of Criticism: Four Essays*, p. 234.

KING OF THE JEWS

Conrad forgets the Nativity. Otherwise, he ransacks the Gospels. With a few notable exceptions, Gospel texts tend to retain some normative power even in Conrad's later work, and in that regard they stand out from all other scriptural allusions. But it is also revealing of Conrad's rhetoric and of his religious sensibilities that two major Gospel texts that dominate the early fiction disappear as Conrad's agnosticism develops. Those two are the Sermon on the Mount and the Crucifixion.

The standard text against hypocrisy, Matthew 23:23-28, is Conrad's standard, too:

Woe unto you, scribes and Pharisees, hypocrites! for ye pay tithe of mint and anise and cummin, and have omitted the weightier matters of the law, judgment, mercy, and faith: these ought ye to have done, and not to leave the other undone. Ye blind guides, which strain at a gnat, and swallow a camel. Woe unto you, scribes and Pharisees, hypocrites! for ye make clean the outside of the cup and of the platter, but within they are full of extortion and excess. Thou blind Pharisee, cleanse first that which is within the cup and platter, that the outside of them may be clean also. Woe unto you, scribes and Pharisees, hypocrites! for ye are like unto whited sepulchres, which indeed appear beautiful outward, but are within full of dead men's bones, and of all uncleanness. Even so ye also outwardly appear righteous unto men, but within ye are full of hypocrisy and iniquity.

Allusions to this ferocious indictment of the scribes and Pharisees appear early and late, in *An Outcast of the Islands*, in *Heart of Darkness*, in *Chance*, in *Victory*.

In *Victory*, Axel Heyst and his Lena have, apparently, just made love for the first time when, after an interlude, Lena asks Heyst why he cannot love her. To divert Lena from this unpleasant subject, Heyst accuses her of picking a quarrel, illustrating the truth of the narrator's remark that "as far as women are concerned he was altogether uninstructed." Then, because "he didn't know what to say," Heyst adds, "'I don't even understand what I have done or left undone to distress you like this'" (p. 222). It is, of course, the weightier matters of faith and love that Heyst, as he well knows despite his disclaimer, has left undone. His dead men's bones are his father's words, the scribe he had been rereading during the interlude. Evidently, Matthew's text is on Heyst's mind in his penultimate words. He uses Jesus' prefatory damnation (repeated eight times in the chapter's thirty-nine verses) when he says to Davidson of those weightier matters, "'Woe to the man whose heart has not learned while young to hope, to love—and to put his trust in life!'" (p. 410). The corpses of Jones and Ricardo reiterate the text. Ricardo, "'the unclean ruffian,'" rots in the sun. Jones is found wrapped in his gorgeous blue dressing gown (see Matt. 23:5), "'like a heap of bones in a blue silk bag'" (p. 411). Although Conrad parodies many other scriptures in *Victory*, this one seems to keep its dignity intact,

84

suggesting that Heyst no less than Ricardo and Jones is "full of hypocrisy and iniquity." It hardly redeems Heyst that he blames his father. The worst irony of Heyst's penultimate words is that he has learned nothing. Pharisees, as Jesus expressly points out, habitually blame their fathers (Matt. 23:30–32).

Marlow in *Chance* uses another verse from this text against Mrs. Fyne, another naïve hypocrite with a father to blame. The long second chapter that finally launches us into the saga of the Fynes and Flora ends with the following paragraph representative of Marlow's ethos in *Chance:*

I had always wondered how she occupied her time. It was in writing. Like her husband, she too published a little book. It had nothing to do with pedestrianism. It was a sort of handbook for women with grievances (and all women had them), a sort of compendious theory and practice of feminine free morality. . . . I marvelled to myself at her complete ignorance of the world, of her own sex, and of other kind of sinners. Yet, where could she have got any experience? Her father had kept her strictly cloistered. Marriage with Fyne was certainly a change, but only to another claustration. You may tell me that the ordinary powers of observation ought to have been enough. Why, yes! But, then, as she had set up for a guide and teacher, there was nothing surprising for me in the discovery that she was blind. That's quite in order. [Pp. 65–66]

Mrs. Fyne, then, is another blind guide, another Pharisee (see also Matt. 15:14). But surely this rhetoric exceeds the bounds of sense. The allusion says less about Mrs. Fyne than it says about Marlow. He is the blind guide of *Chance.* John A. Palmer regrets Marlow's pomposity, his "condescension and contempt," his "unpleasantness," and Palmer incisively enumerates Marlow's shortcomings and contradictions. It is of some interest that Palmer finds "hypocrisy" to be not the least of Marlow's defects. Palmer also rightly cites Marlow's naïve analyses and his "figures of speech wholly dissociated from their context." These failures make *Chance* a bad novel because, Palmer claims, Marlow is Conrad, if only "an incomplete projection."[1] More recently William Bonney, ignoring such objections as Palmer raises, also makes Marlow Conrad's man who speaks for ontic emptiness, a consistency Bonney constructs in the teeth of his affection for discontinuity.[2] Palmer's list of defects is so long and convincing, however, that it seems incredible to make those defects signs of aesthetic failure, to ascribe them to chance alone. Conrad's epigraph should caution us against that. If we renounce the assumption that Marlow speaks for Conrad, the charge of aesthetic failure loses its force, at least upon the grounds of *Marlow's* unpleasantness and manifest contradictions.

Marlow's scriptural rhetoric is so flagrantly dense that it must signal a huge dramatic irony. He is a variant on the piety of the old professor of *Under Western Eyes,* pagan worshiper of chance who habitually perceives and evaluates his world by the light of the English Bible. Marlow makes the mixed metaphors, not Flora or de Barral or Anthony or Powell. It is Marlow who contrasts de Barral with the preacher of vanity and Marlow who puts him under Anthony's heel (pp. 84, 298, 432–44; see chapter 2 above). The symbolic contradiction is Marlow's. Like Madame de S——, Marlow has the Exodus on his brain, feeling that "'the days of wonders and portents had not passed away yet,'" speaking

[1] John A. Palmer, *Joseph Conrad's Fiction*, pp. 200–204.

[2] William W. Bonney, *Thorns & Arabesques: Contexts for Conrad's Fiction*, pp. 96–107. Bonney, however, begins with the caveat that "it is not possible legitimately to discuss anything in *Chance* but what the 'I' says. There are no characters or events as they are customarily conceived" (p. 97).

of Zoe Fyne's "'days of bondage'" and Mrs. de Barral's "days of exile" (68, 71; see also p. 74). But Marlow's most precious Old Testament text is Daniel's sign and portent of the end of Israel's subjugation, the pollution of the temple in Jerusalem: "And arms shall stand on his part, and they shall pollute the sanctuary of strength, and shall take away the daily sacrifice, and they shall place the abomination that maketh desolate" (Dan. 11:31; see also Matt. 24:15). "Abominable" is Marlow's pet adjective: a drizzle is "abominable" (p. 85); Charlie is "an abominable scamp" (pp. 95, 101); the governess is always "abominable," "an abomination" (pp. 104, 140, 232, 263, 335); de Barral's East End relatives practice "abominable vulgarity" (p. 163); Marlow calls his rooms "an abominable hole" (p. 137); outside the hotel, Marlow sees "three abominable, drink-sodden loafers" (p. 230), and Smith uses the word "abominable" three times before he tries to poison Anthony (p. 408); the poison itself is an "abominable weapon" (p. 437); the entire world is "abominable" (p. 364). Marlow's penchant for this distinctive adjective is not the only argument for Daniel's temple. These fourteen instances of the adjective are satellites, their erratic orbits wheeling about Marlow's explicit allusion when he describes the end of Flora's innocence: "The end came in the abomination of desolation of the poor child's miserable cry for help" (p. 122). Flora is the polluted temple. And Marlow is quite aware of his metaphor. Prophetlike, he foretells the end when he warns us that Flora's "unconsciousness was to be broken into with profane violence, with desecrating circumstances, like a temple violated by a mad, vengeful impiety" (p. 99).[3] Surely

[3] Thus two planes of allusion intersect, the biblical joining that to Tasso's *Gerusaleme liberata*. See Bonney, *Thorns & Arabesques*, pp. 96–104; and Gerald H. Levin, "An Allusion to Tasso in Conrad's *Chance*," *NCF* 13 (September, 1958):145–51.

Conrad expects his readers' trust in Marlow to be desolated by his preposterous metaphor. Marlow is the blind guide, the Pharisee.

Conrad puts these allusions into the mouth of Marlow so as to disassociate himself from his creature. Marlow does not speak for Conrad. But he does speak of Conrad. Actually, I am only rearranging Palmer's argument. Conrad laughs at Marlow just as Marlow laughs at the Fynes. In *Chance*, *Victory*, and *The Rescue*, Conrad is as distant from his characters as they are from one another. The aesthetic accomplishments of *Chance*, as well as those of *Victory* and *The Rescue*, are considerable. The temple metaphor *is* beautifully done, for example, as are the novel's unplumbable narrative ironies. Conrad treats us to a delightful paradox: a novel that purports to be about the workings of chance is constructed with high artifice, its plot and skeins of imagery as intricate as those of *The Ambassadors*. But it has not the least trace of James's compassionate toleration for or passionate understanding of humankind. What is unsettling about *Chance*, and about *Victory*, is its mixture of structural beauty and moral insufficiency. Conrad builds a temple for Circe's changelings. He—not Marlow, not Mrs. Fyne—is the Pharisee, *Chance* his whited sepulchre.

The moral distinction between Conrad early and Conrad late can be seen in his manner of using the evangelist's text in *An Outcast of the Islands*, by standard aesthetic criteria a novel far inferior to *Chance*. Like Heyst, Willems blames his sins upon others. When Lingard confronts Willems after he has smashed King Tom's promised land, Willems cries out, "'It wasn't me. The evil was not in me'" (p. 273). To see Willems as another white man seduced by the wiles of tropical ways is to see him as Willems desires. He even stoops to a common biblical figure to lard his plea: "'I was alone in that infernal savage crowd. I was delivered into their hands'" (p. 274). Willems may hope that Lingard hears Luke's variant, "Let these sayings sink down into your ears: for the Son of man shall be delivered into the hands of men" (9:44). This passage contrasts neatly with Willems earlier thought out of Matthew. Willems "had, for a moment, a wicked pleasure in the thought that what he had done could not be undone. He had given himself up. He felt proud of it" (p. 127). Lingard almost unmixes the metaphor when he is "angry at what Willems had done—and also angry about what he had left undone" (p. 202). But Conrad grants Willems a moment of insight, the kind of moment he denies to Heyst in *Victory* and to Marlow in *Chance*. Willems, in an instant of conversion that passes as suddenly as it comes, sees the whited sepulchre: "And, all at once, it seemed to him that he was peering into a sombre hollow, into a black hole full of decay and of whitened bones; into an immense and inevitable grave full of corruption where sooner or later he must, unavoidably, fall" (p. 339). Now Willems has "a disgusted horror of himself," a Kurtzlike insight. Assuming the fetal position—"He drew his feet up, his head sank between his shoulders, his arms hugged his sides"—he nestles "in the darkness of his own making" (p. 342). At this auspicious moment of revelation when Willems is reborn a moral person, Joanna arrives with their child, and Willems's dark knowledge dissipates with the morning fog. Transient it may be, but it is genuine nonetheless. Early Conrad allows that authentic freedom is possible even for a wretch like Willems. Late Conrad does not, even for a "superior person" like Axel Heyst. In the late novels (excluding *The Rover*), a character's moment of self-knowledge is his moment of greatest self-deception.

Or, finally, compare the Marlow of *Chance* with the Marlow of *Heart of Darkness.* He too repeats the text from Matthew, but in *Heart of Darkness* it has high ethical meaning, the standard by which we evaluate the rapacious hypocrisies of colonialism and the milder hypocrisies of Marlow. I have in mind Marlow's words about the European capital where his adventure starts, "'a city that always makes me think of a whited sepulchre'" (p. 55). Colonialism has made Africa and therefore Europe itself into that whited sepulchre full of dead men's bones and of all uncleanness. The sepulchre holds Fresleven's bones (p. 54) and the ports of call "where the merry dance of death and trade goes on in a still and earthy atmosphere as of an overheated catacomb" (p. 62); it holds the black bones in the grove of death marked with white worsted (pp. 66–67), and it holds Kurtz, "an animated image of death carved out of old ivory" (p. 134). The tale's trail of white-on-black images begins and ends at Matthew's text. Wherever Marlow goes, he is in the whited sepulchre. Kurtz went out an evangelical capitalist believing (if we can believe the strawless brickmaker) that "'each station should be like a beacon on the road to better things, a centre for trade, of course, but also for humanizing, improving, instructing'" (p. 91). Kurtz, or the brickmaker, mimics Isaiah's missionary text (40:3–5), a text repeated in each of the synoptic Gospels to describe the Baptist: "Prepare ye the way of the Lord, make straight in the desert a highway for our God. Every valley shall be exalted, and every mountain and hill shall be made low: and the crooked shall be made straight, and the rough places plain: And the glory of the Lord shall be revealed, and all flesh shall see it together: for the mouth of the Lord hath spoken it." Marlow's charming aunt foists the same evangelical mission upon her nephew: "I was to be one of the Workers, with a capital—you know. Something like an emissary of light, something like a lower sort of apostle." Then Charlie's aunt speaks the appropriate text to rebut Marlow's demur that "the Company was run for profit": "'You forget, dear Charlie, that the labourer is worthy of his hire'" (p. 59). These are Jesus' words to the seventy lower apostles whom he sends out "as lambs among wolves" to preach that "the kingdom of God is come nigh unto you" (Luke 10:1–11). So Marlow goes off to live out his boyish dream among the wolves of profit and progress. But not as a lamb. Marlow takes care to impress his auditors aboard the *Nellie* with the contrast between his aunt's airy innocence and his own perspicacity. Marlow has a pharisaic taint. After all, for the sake of a boy's imagination he eagerly collaborates in an obscenity. He knows that the evangelistic fervor is "rot," its motive "profit" (p. 59). Perhaps he conceitedly disparages his aunt's illusions because he is desperate, even on the *Nellie* after a lapse of years, to preserve his illusions about himself. After leaving his aunt, Marlow tells his auditors, he stood in the street with "the queer feeling" that he "was an impostor" (p. 60). Conrad may have taken inspiration for his title from another text about hypocrisy, one about people "who became vain in their imaginations, and their foolish heart was darkened" (Rom. 1:21). Yet in the final scene with the Intended that echoes the parting with his aunt, Marlow learns something about the foolishness of his imagination, as we shall see.

In *Heart of Darkness* and *An Outcast of the Islands,* then, Conrad uses Matthew's text as a moral guide. In *Chance* it merely makes Marlow ridiculous, its import merely epistemological, indicating that our guide is blind. But the question in *Chance* is whether the blind are leading the blind, whether Conrad tumbles into the ditch.

The ferocious Gospel figure whom early Conrad takes as a standard against hypocrisy, as a model of perfect fidelity, is John the Baptist, the voice in the wilderness preparing the way of the Lord, making paths straight (Matt. 3:3; Mark 1:3; Luke 3:3-6). The Baptist provides an ironic contrast by which we may judge fidelities in *Nostromo, Heart of Darkness,* and *The Secret Agent.*

Early in *Nostromo* we are pointedly reminded of the symbolism in the titular character's true name. The casa Viola ringed about, Teresa cries, "'Oh Gian' Battista,'" and the narrator interprets: "She was not invoking the saint himself, but calling upon Nostromo, whose patron he was" (p. 17). Nostromo, "a fellow in a thousand," "'absolutely above reproach'" (pp. 12-13), is not the "horn of salvation" sent "to give light to them that sit in darkness" (Luke 1:69, 79; see also John 5:35). In fact, the light appalls Nostromo. Conrad may be thinking of Luke's text when Nostromo first sees the lighthouse going up: "It was dark. Not every man had such a darkness. And they were going to put a light there. A light!" (p. 525). The irony is less subtle when, Nostromo having resolved to "grow rich very slowly," Conrad pronounces his full name for the first time, "Gian' Battista Fidanza" (p. 502). Even as the silver bears down more heavily upon Nostromo, so does the irony. In his first love scene with Giselle she addresses him repeatedly in his patron's name, sewing an altar cloth the while (pp. 533-39).

Kurtz is another voice crying in the wilderness, but it may be a sign of Marlow's moral growth that he does not mistake Kurtz for the *vox clamantis.* The simile he twice uses for the helmsman, the second time to compare him with Kurtz, suggests his perception: "He had no restraint, no restraint—just like Kurtz—a tree swayed by the wind"

(p. 119; see also p. 110). Jesus praises John's steadfastness when he asks John's disciples, "What went ye out into the wilderness for to see? A reed shaken with the wind?" (Luke 7:24). The allusion contrasts John's fidelity with Kurtz's fall. "Paths, paths, everywhere; a stamped-in network of paths," Marlow observes, as he sets off for the Central Station, "down and up chilly ravines, up and down stony hills ablaze with heat" (p. 70). Kurtz has not made the crooked straight or the rough places plain. Instead of a beheaded prophet, Marlow finds a beheading Herod.

In *The Secret Agent,* John's daemons are Michaelis and the Professor, voices crying in an urban wilderness. Michaelis is an "Apostle," Marx his Christ, his faith in economic determinism growing "like a faith revealed in visions," "like an act of grace" (pp. 44, 45). The "martyrdom" of this "hermit of visions in the desert of a penitentiary" consists in being forbidden "all access to the healing waters" of a spa (pp. 42, 50). Instead of locusts and honey, Michaelis feeds on "raw carrots and milk" (p. 303). The Professor has a touch of the prophet too. The man who had defiantly declared, "'What do we want with refuges?'" soon takes comfort in remembering "the refuge of his room, . . . lost in a wilderness of poor houses" (pp. 73, 82). He is another preacher's son, early indoctrinated into the enthusiasms of an "obscure but rigid Christian sect" (p. 80). Although the "science of colleges" replaces "the faith of conventicles" in the son, the essential "moral attitude" remains, "translated . . . into a frenzied puritanism of ambition," "something secularly holy" (pp. 80–81). The Gospel figure retains his integrity. But the evangelical capitalism of *Heart of Darkness,* the careers of Holroyd and Father Corbelan in *Nostromo,* and the Professor's biography all insinuate that institutional Christianity helps degrade the values of its founding text.

Conrad repeatedly echoes a major discourse on those values, the Sermon on the Mount. Even weak echoes are worth remarking because they can illuminate the distinction between Conrad early and late, between agnosticism and atheism.

"Daily bread" is one example. Conrad serves it up often in his later work. The tenors for this vehicle range from literary criticism (*Personal Record,* p. 96) to "sugar" ("A Smile of Fortune," p. 3). It is also "actualities" (*Chance,* p. 87), a sign of a slave (*Victory,* p. 150), fish ("Poland Revisited," p. 158; "Tradition," p. 194), and simply food ("Confidence," p. 204). Were it not such a cliché, one might say that Conrad's sundry uses empty it of meaning. But it is a cliché, already empty. Yet later Conrad takes care that it remains empty. Three early uses of the expression breathe some life into it. One is in "The End of the Tether," where it effectively resumes Whalley's life and character: "All the days of his life he had prayed, for daily bread, and not to be led into temptation, in a childlike humility of spirit" (p. 325). The other two uses are in *Lord Jim.* Marlow is referring to Jim's episodic career between the *Patna* and Patusan—nouns containing a hint, probably fortuitous, of the Latin *panis:* "To fling away your daily bread so as to get your hands free for a grapple with a ghost may be an act of prosaic heroism" (p. 197). Marlow curiously echoes our initial narrator on Jim's career before the *Patna:* "he had to bear the prosaic severity of the daily task that gives bread" (p. 10). But Lord Jim wants transubstantiation. He flings away prosaic bread to become a holy ghost, "a disembodied spirit astray amongst the passions of this earth, ready to surrender himself faithfully to the claim of his own world of shades" (p. 416). These uses of the cliché invigorate it with multiple and elusive meanings. The later Conrad's reiterated and random significances neutralize it.

Substantial uses of the Sermon appear, however, in early Conrad, most notably in *Nostromo* and *The Secret Agent.* In any death scene in Conrad you are likely to hear Scripture, and Nostromo at his death naïvely repeats Jesus' classic text against materialism:

> Lay not up for yourselves treasures upon earth, where moth and rust doth corrupt, and where thieves break through and steal: But lay up for yourselves treasures in heaven, where neither moth nor rust doth corrupt, and where thieves do not break through nor steal: For where your treasure is, there will your heart be also. [Matt. 6:19–21]

Behind the multiple uses of "treasure" in *Nostromo* looms this text. Antonia Avellanos grafts Matthew 6:12 onto 6:21 when she says to Charles Gould during the "exodus": " 'Forgive us our misery! It is your character that is the inexhaustible treasure that may save us all yet' " (p. 361). Her heart entombed in the mine, Mrs. Gould has a "prophetic vision" of herself "all alone in the Treasure House of the world" (p. 522), conflating Matthew 5:14 and 6:21. The narrator observes that "Sulaco had outstripped Nostromo's prudence, growing rich swiftly on the hidden treasure of the earth" and then that Dr. Monygham lived "on the inexhaustible treasure of his devotion drawn upon in the secret of his heart" (p. 504). Everyone in *Nostromo* misreads the text. There is a lovely irony in the twice-used "inexhaustible." Gould's character, the silver in the mine and the silver buried on Great Isabel, and the doctor's devotion prove exhausting. Nostromo suffers most for his misreading, for he becomes both the thief who breaks through and the thief's victim. "'Like a thief!'" Nostromo exclaims, and with pitiless dramatic irony Conrad has Viola say, thinking that he has shot Ramirez, "'Like a thief he came, and like a thief he fell'" (p. 554). Another thief in the night. This skein of imagery is wound up when Mrs. Gould comes to shrive Nostromo, "monastically hooded" like the confessor Nostromo would not fetch for the dying Teresa (p. 558). Mrs. Gould confesses, "'I, too, have hated the idea of that silver from the bottom of my heart,'" and Nostromo replies:

"Marvelous!—that one of you should hate the wealth that you know so well how to take from the hands of the poor. The world rests upon the poor, as old Giorgio says. You have always been good to the poor. But there is something accursed in wealth. Senora, shall I tell you where the treasure is? To you alone? . . . Shining! Incorruptible!" [P. 560]

"Where your treasure is, there will your heart be also," and Nostromo's heart is to the end with his corrupting, corruptible treasure. We may perhaps excuse Nostromo if, in his last extremity, he is not listening to Mrs. Gould. It is not the silver itself but the idea of the silver that she detests. Except for Emilia Gould, everyone in *Nostromo* forgets, even as Chaucer's Pardoner forgets, the exact reading of another text, that not money itself but "the love of money is the root of all evil" (1 Tim. 6:10). The Pardoner's three thieves betray one another and find spiritual death at the root of a tree. Nostromo feels inexplicably "betrayed," betrays himself, and finds "'death come . . . upon [him] unawares'" at the root of the tree where his treasure is (p. 559). Conrad's tale is Chaucer's, with the difference that Conrad's world does not admit redemption.

At the root of a tree in *The Secret Agent* are the mangled

remains of the innocent Stevie, blown up by the bomb of the Professor, who preaches a mangled version of the Sermon on the Mount to Comrade Ossipon. The Professor heaps scorn upon Michaelis's dream "'of a world planned out like an immense and nice hospital, with gardens and flowers, in which the strong are to devote themselves to the care of the weak.'" Michaelis may have been reading *The Dark Night of the Soul* (2.16.10).[4] That John the Professor loathes, for against Paul and Jesus, he preaches that the love of the weak is the root of all evil:

> Conceive you this folly, Ossipon? The weak! The source of all evil on this earth! . . . I told him that I dreamt of a world like shambles, where the weak would be taken in hand for utter extermination.
> "Do you understand, Ossipon? The source of all evil! They are our sinister masters—the weak, the flabby, the silly, the cowardly, the faint of heart, and the slavish of mind. They have power. They are the multitude. Theirs is the kingdom of the earth. Exterminate! Exterminate! That is the only way of progress. It is! Follow me, Ossipon. First the great multitude of the weak must go, then only the relatively strong. You see? First the blind, then the deaf and dumb, then the halt and the lame—and so on. Every taint, every vice, every prejudice must meet its doom."
> [P. 303]

The Professor's speech is one of Conrad's more brilliant revisions of Scripture. He practices for it in *An Outcast of the Islands,* where Willems explains to his club friends the secret of his extraordinary rise above the "shabby multitude" of de Souzas whom he feeds (p. 4): "Those are the

---

[4] A year after *The Secret Agent* was published, Conrad received a copy of Mrs. Graham's translation, probably in July or August, 1907. See Joseph Conrad, *Joseph Conrad's Letters to Cunninghame Graham*, ed. C. T. Watts, pp. 172-73.

fools, the weak, the contemptible. The wise, the strong, the respected have no scruples. Where there are scruples there can be no power. On that text he preached often" (p. 8). His text, and the Professor's, is the Sermon on the Mount turned inside out. They invert the Pater Noster and the Beatitudes, as any up-and-coming capitalist or perfect anarchist ought to do. The Professor goes even further, in one speech managing to pervert the course of Jesus' ministry.

In the chapter immediately preceding the Sermon, Jesus says to Peter and Andrew as the Professor to Ossipon, "Follow me," and Jesus heals "all manner of sickness and all manner of disease among the people" (Matt. 4:19, 23). Through Jesus, "The blind receive their sight, and the lame walk, the lepers are cleansed, and the deaf hear" (Matt. 11:5). But the Professor is the messiah of dynamite who aims "'to break up the superstition and worship of legality'" and sneers, "'Prophecy! What's the good of thinking of what will be!'" (pp. 73, 306), unlike Jesus, who tells the "multitude" gathered at the Mount that he has not "come to destroy the law, or the prophets" (Matt. 5:17). Instead of acknowledging that the kingdom and power belong to God (Matt. 6:13), the Professor attributes them to "the poor in spirit" and the "meek" (Matt. 5:3, 5). His dream of carnage has already come to pass in the destruction of Stevie, who stands for all the weak and meek of the earth, for the "multitude" at the Mount. Jesus calls them "the salt of the earth" (Matt. 5:13); for Winnie, Stephen had been "what there was of the salt of passion in her tasteless life" (p. 174). Winnie's end completes Jesus' text: ". . . but if the salt have lost his savour, wherewith shall it be salted? it is thenceforth good for nothing, but to be cast out, and to be trodden under foot of men." Like Jesus, or the Authorized scholars, Conrad puns on "saviour" with Winnie's Tom

Ossipon, who, true to her vow, puts her head under his feet (pp. 291–96). The multitude dies, and Winnie, when Stevie stumbles in the park.

A passage in Conrad's Preface to *The Secret Agent,* written thirteen years after the novel, suggests that he still heard his garbled echoes. As he does in his Preface to the *Youth* volume, Conrad identifies his primary scripture for us. Of London he writes: "Then a vision of an enormous town presented itself, a monstrous town more populous than some continents and in its man-made might as if indifferent to heaven's frowns and smiles; a cruel devourer of the world light" (p. xxvi). Conrad's "frowns and smiles" may recast Jesus' words about the sun and rain from heaven (Matt. 5:45). The combined images of the city and "the world's light" certainly echo Jesus' second metaphor for the multitude, "Ye are the light of the world. A city that is set on a hill cannot be hid" (Matt. 5:14). But in *The Secret Agent* the "man-made might" of the secular city devours the spiritual "light of the world."

The action of the novel begins, in fact, with a contrast between secular and spiritual cities established by an allusion to the rusted treasures of the earth that moth and rust corrupt. With an irony more bitter than a metaphysical poet's, Conrad puns upon the "London sun" that "glorified" the "opulence and luxury" Verloc beholds as he walks westward to Mr. Vladimir. With "an air of punctual and benign vigilance" this sun casts "an old-gold tinge in [its] diffused light," as the multitude is told to let its "light so shine before men, that they may see your good works, and glorify your Father which is in heaven" (Matt. 5:16). But the secret agent Verloc is not inclined to let anyone see his good works. This secular sun produces "a dull effect of rustiness" over all, including Verloc's back. Verloc, of course, is "not in the least conscious of having got rusty" (pp. 11, 12). The secret agent Verloc might have been spared some discomfort had he been conscious of the moral Jesus makes of the rusty treasure: "No man can serve two masters" (Matt. 6:24).

Daniel Schwarz has remarked that the imagery of Verloc's walk may be derived from Donne, and that is certainly possible, though it is also possible that Donne and Conrad share the same source. Schwarz sees some hope in allusions to Genesis, Homer, and Shakespeare in *The Secret Agent,* that they raise "the possibility that London's moral darkness may be temporary."[5] But Schwarz notes neither the Sermon nor the writing on the wall. I can extract very little comfort from either of those two dominant metaphors. The light seems utterly devoured, the writing erased to "nothing." The "holes in space and time" that Conrad describes in connection with Heat's pursuit of anarchists (p. 85) describe the image of history that *The Secret Agent* implies. History does not reveal linear or cyclic growth or development or purpose. Theories of causation are of no account. Each civilization is absolutely divorced from its predecessors. Conrad's agnostic conception of history is idiosyncratic. On the one hand, the light and the wall are authentic metaphors of moral and spiritual realities. Conrad grants their meaningfulness at one time. The import of *The Secret Agent,* and of *Nostromo,* depends upon positing a prior validity in the images of the sacred text. So strong is this supposition that *The Secret Agent* might not be uncongenial reading to members of the Professor's rigid Christian sect. A disgust for the material world pervades the novel, and Conrad seems to react with pessimistic fervor against the seculari-

[5] Daniel R. Schwarz, *Conrad: "Almayer's Folly" to "Under Western Eyes,"* pp. 171–74.

zation of Providence and the degradation of the Christian idea of liberty. On the other hand, *The Secret Agent* offers no alternative, neither the wrath to come nor a reward in heaven. What I sense is not a theory of decline from the sacred standard but a theory of radical discontinuity. Ultimately the scriptures of *The Secret Agent* argue that the ladder of Jacob and Jesus is less than dust. Now the sacred text has merely negative value, signifying emptiness. History is a wilderness of mirrors reflecting nothing. In the light of the London sun "neither wall, nor tree, nor beast, nor man cast a shadow" (p. 11).

We can reconstruct the Passion from the Last Supper to the Resurrection by culling texts from Conrad. Mr. Vladimir and Peter Ivanovitch commemorate the woman who anointed Jesus (Matt. 26:11-13): "'Murder is always with us,'" Vladimir tells Verloc; Peter Ivanovitch, with two apostles in his name, tells Razumov: "'Verily, without women we can do nothing. So it stands written, and apparently so it is'" (pp. 239-40). Hearing Karl Yundt talk about "'eating people's flesh and drinking their blood'" sends Stevie into one of his fits about the remission of sins. Winnie's apt question sums up the scriptural rhetoric of *The Secret Agent:* "'What's the good of talking like that?'" (p. 51; Matt. 26:26-29). Jones makes a joke of Jesus' rebuke of the sleeping disciples (Matt. 26:41) when he says to the watchful Ricardo, "'Watch, eh? Why not pray a little, too?'" (p. 334). But the joke is on Jones, for Ricardo has already entered into temptation. Conrad completes Jones's verse many times—for example, inverting it in "Poland Revisited" to mourn mankind's mechanization, "Its spirit is apparently so weak now, and its flesh has grown so strong" (*Notes,* p. 163), and in a letter (August 24, 1895) to E. L. Sanderson, "Flesh is weak; and the spirit of little account."[6] Willems reenacts the agony and silence in the garden when he surrenders to the seductions of Aissa one night in the forest. After hearing "a far-off voice—the voice of his fate," he feels a "rending and tearing within his breast. . . . On his forehead the perspiration stood out in small pearly drops. . . . Round him there was a great silence. . . . This silence, this immobility of his surroundings, seemed to him a cold rebuke, a stern refusal, a cruel unconcern." Then Willems surrenders "the unstained purity of his life" (p. 80; Luke 22:39-46).

With Victor Haldin and Razumov we leave the garden. Sending Razumov to arrange an escape on the sledge of the drunkard, Ziemianitch, Haldin says, "as though he were talking in his sleep," "'The time has come to put fate to the test. . . . Go with God, thou silent soul'" (p. 24). The professor of languages translates us into another lovely dramatic irony: "Sleep on now, and take your rest: it is enough, the hour is come; behold, the Son of man is betrayed into the hands of sinners. Rise up, let us go; lo, he that betrayeth me is at hand" (Mark 14:41-42). After he beats the drunkard, Razumov, Son of reason, does just that. There is dramatic irony through allusion again in *Lord Jim*, where Marlow slightly alters Jesus' rebuke of the disciple who commits hubris by cutting off an ear. Marlow sums up Jim's career by saying, "Who toys with the sword shall perish by the sword" (p. 342). Changing the verb of the Authorized Version from "take" to "toys" (Matt. 26:52) distinguishes true hubris from Jim's manifold illusion.

Judas is active in Conrad, a model not only for Razumov but also for Cornelius in *Lord Jim*, for Ossipon when he tries to foist his legacy upon the Professor (pp. 309-10;

---

[6]G. Jean-Aubry, *Joseph Conrad: Life and Letters*, 1:176.

Matt. 27:3–5), and in her father's, or Marlow's, fevered imagination for Flora in *Chance* (p. 364). Pilate appears in the form of the chubby and pious Shaw of *The Rescue*. Giving up Lingard, Shaw "'washed his hands of everything'" (p. 291). But Marlow "could not think of washing [his] hands" of Jim (p. 200). Shaw justifies laving his hands, because, according to Carter, "'evil communications [corrupt] good manners.'" Just as he does with the thief in the night, Conrad begs us to open the Bible. Carter continues: "'Seems to me I've heard that before. Queer thing to say'" (p. 229). He has heard it in Conrad's favorite Epistle, 1 Corinthians (15:33). Paul refers to those who doubt the Resurrection.[7] *The Rescue* is not for those who take no pleasure in scriptural rhetoric. For Lingard is eventually made to mime the resurrection after the *Emma* blows up. D'Alcacer is Mary Magdalene to Lingard's Jesus: "'Don't disturb me, Mr. d'Alcacer. I have just come back to life'" (p. 444; John 20:17).[8]

This sampling is representative of the change in Conrad's rhetoric. Later allusions to the Passion are cunningly contrived, usually extended. Earlier allusions seem to be spontaneous responses to the emotion of the moment, like the allusions to the Epistles in the Preface to *The Nigger*. This change from spontaneity to artifice may be owing to a change in the quality of Conrad's agnosticism: the more thoroughly agnostic he becomes, perhaps even to atheism, the more numerous and contrived are the allusions. Once

---

[7] While he was revising the completed draft of *The Rescue*, Conrad wrote to Curle, "Isn't it written (in the correspondence of the Apostles, I believe) that 'literary communications corrupt good manners'?" Joseph Conrad, *Conrad to a Friend: 150 Selected Letters from Joseph Conrad to Richard Curle*, ed. Richard Curle, p. 44.

[8] Bonney, *Thorns*, p. 147.

the text has been drained of its sacred prerogatives, Conrad can manipulate it as he chooses. But matters may be more complex than that. The proliferation of highly elaborate scriptural metaphors that begins at a canter with *The Secret Agent* and gallops to *The Rescue* has about it ample hints of anxiety. Conrad is too eager to lay this ghost to rest, too obsessed with neutralizing Scripture. The obsession tacitly credits the sacred text with the meaningfulness that Conrad ostensibly denies. Perhaps that meaning is psychological, Scripture an indissoluble part of Conrad's sense of himself as a writer of English fiction. Conrad drains himself as he tries to drain Scripture. Hence the contempt that pervades *Chance, Victory,* and *The Rescue.*

It may say something about the relationship of Conrad's idea of himself to the English Bible that all save one of his undoubted allusions to the Crucifixion appear in his early work, and there commonly. The exception is a brief potshot in *Chance.* After the "abominable" governess and her "abominable scamp" desert, Flora "called out twice 'Papa! Papa!'" and then "everything about her became quite still" (p. 123). No one offers vinegar, and the stillness reverses Matthew's account of a quaking earth, but Marlow's phrase recalls the evangelist's: "And about the ninth hour Jesus cried with a loud voice, saying, Eli, Eli" (27:46). If it is an echo, it is a quiet one, not at all like the "abomination of desolation" or Shaw's "'evil communications'" or Lingard's thief in the night that cry their source from the housetops. Perhaps the climax of the Passion still had sufficient claims upon Conrad that he could not subvert it. His earlier echoes of the crucifixion are not subversions, and they are certainly loud enough.

Compare Flora's cry with Yanko's death in "Amy Foster" or Kayerts's in "An Outpost of Progress." There's no doubt that Yanko imitates Christ, he a creature of light and air rejected by the earthy Pharisees of Colebrook. "'Water! Give me water!'" Yanko cries (John 19:28). Amy deserts, to hear Yanko "call out twice after her down the road in a terrible voice." At his death, "The spear of the hunter . . . entered his very soul" (pp. 140–41; Matt. 27:46). His Mary gets a John, too (p. 142). Conrad's touch here is in no sense light. Nor is it an "An Outpost" when Kayerts hangs himself upon the gigantic cross erected over the grave of the station's mysterious first master. As he goes on his way to the cross (he had "lost his way"), Kayerts sees it in the thickening fog as a "smudge," a "stain" (p. 116). The cross had sagged "much out of the perpendicular" before Kayerts's fellow pioneer and eventual accidental victim, Carlier, "replanted the cross firmly," not out of piety but because, he says, "'it used to make me squint, leaning over so much. So I just planted it upright. And solid. I promise you'" (pp. 87, 95). Thus the righted cross becomes an efficient instrument for suicide. The point, I gather, is that Christianity righted would not partake in the African progress.

Kurtz too "cried out twice," not in a loud voice but in "a cry that was no more than a breath—"'The horror! The horror!'" If Kurtz's "'horror'" recollects Abram's theophany, we come even closer, to "'Eli, Eli.'" Just before he cries out, Conrad gives us a certain allusion. Watching Kurtz's face change was, says Marlow, "as though a veil had been rent," as the "veil of the temple was rent in twain" (Matt. 27:51; p. 149). Perhaps Conrad emulates a familiar paradox. Perhaps "'the horror'" means that Kurtz renounces the metaphysical desire that had undone him and, in renouncing, comes to a true imitation of Christ. But such a reading would perch Conrad awkwardly atop a mystic mountain. Marlow makes the allusion, and it therefore characterizes him, not Kurtz. The allusion may signify that Marlow is infected, too, his illness on the trip down river as much metaphysical as real. Marlow returns to "the sepulchral city" (p. 152) his imagination diseased, another Gulliver disgusted with his own kind, convinced of his own righteousness. He goes to the Intended full of evangelistic fervor, ready to restrain the darkness, "to keep [it] back alone for the salvation of another soul" (p. 156). But Marlow's contact with unaffected, if deluded, human love seems to save him instead. Her grief purges his hubris. Marlow realizes that "I could not have defended her—. . . . I could not even defend myself" (p. 159). Marlow is brought to a secular renunciation of singularity, acknowledging his own part in the making of darkness.

If Kurtz renounces metaphysical desire, he is extraordinary. Conrad's messiahs usually do not know their disease, much less have the will to renounce it. The first four chapters of *Lord Jim* diagnose the messianic virus in Jim's romanticism. Like Willems with the de Souzas, Jim craves the role of savior, the providential man "destined to shine" (p. 5). The *Patna* is the right ship for his unconscious desire, carrying pilgrims "urged by the faith and the hope of paradise," lured by "the promise of salvation, the reward of eternal life" (pp. 9, 13). But Jim fails as suffering Christ. He comes down from his cross. Recounting his last minutes on board while the white officers exhort the dead George to jump into their boat, Jim exclaims, "'Eight hundred living people, and they were yelling to the one dead man to come down and be saved!'" (p. 68). The preacher's son may recall the mockers of Christ, "'. . . save thyself. If thou be the Son of God, come down from the cross'" (Matt. 27:40). Jim says that, after his fall, the men in the boat reviled him as if he were "'a tree'd thief'" (p. 72), but which of the

106

two thieves Jim has in mind I cannot guess.[9] Jim can come
to terms with his failings only by giving them a scriptural
gloss, and he seems ingenuously blind to the true object of
his desire suggested by his allusions.

In all these instances Conrad credits the Crucifixion
with moral, perhaps even sacred, value. Nothing can be
rent or stained that has not been sole or unspotted. We are
too plainly meant to sympathize with Yanko-Christ. The
hubris of a Kurtz or a Jim is hubris only by contrast. These
four crucifixions are, therefore, in essence tame and conservative imitations. But they prepare the way for the radical
imitation in *Nostromo*, the death of "the enterprising Isra-
elite."

A more innocent sufferer for the sins of others does not
appear in modern fiction. Nor is there a more agnostic
Crucifixion. Reversing Christ, this victim spits "violently"
into the face of his tormentor (p. 449; Mark 15:19). "'*Sangre
de* Dios, Sotillo cries out (p. 449), imitating the centurion
(Mark 15:39) and changing water into blood. The "fractious
Jew," the "treacherous Jew" is framed as on an altar: "The
light of two candles burning before the perpendicular and
breathless immobility of the late Señor Hirsch threw a
gleam afar over land and water, like a signal in the night"
(p. 451). Hirsch is a light to the Gentiles, his signal freedom.
The accidents of strangulation allow Kayerts to stick out "a
swollen tongue at his Managing Director." Kurtz and Yanko
wither from disease. Decoud commits a bathetic suicide.
Nostromo is shot by accident. Hirsch resurrects himself
from an abyss of fear to spit deliberately into the face of
torture. His is the only heroic act in *Nostromo*, the only act

[9]Conrad liked the impenitent one. See Conrad, *Letters*, ed. Watts,
p. 59; and Watts's note on Conrad's other references to the thief, p. 62.

that implies freedom. Here Conrad makes terrible beauty out of the Crucifixion, transforming Scripture utterly.

After Hirsch, perhaps there was nothing more Conrad could do with the Crucifixion. Perhaps that explains why he abandons it until the comparatively small-minded episode in *Chance*. Those two scenes say all that needs saying about the change in Conrad's moral imagination.

Razumov ends tended by the compassionate Tekla, whom our professor of languages renames "the Samaritan." She is the outcast who understands the golden rule. Mindful of that rule, I have tried to be equally compassionate, parading not half of the Gospel allusions in Conrad known to me. Undoubtedly I am ignorant of many others. But the number and weight of the allusions described are sufficient to argue that no work had more impact upon Conrad than the Gospels. In fundamental ways the Gospels mean more to Conrad than to any modernist, including Eliot. They antagonize Conrad, and they attract him. Conrad represents the end of a long literary tradition—the tradition of Shakespeare and Donne, of Blake and Shelley and Browning—of a lively dialogue with the Gospels.

THE DAY OF THE LORD

Like Yeats, Wells, Shaw, and other modernists who grew up in the nineteenth century and flourished in the twentieth, Conrad is given to visions droll and somber of the world's end. As Conrad's agnosticism hardens, the Sermon on the Mount and the Crucifixion are replaced as dominant metaphors by the parable of the king's wedding feast (Matt. 22:1–14; Luke 14:16–24), apocalyptic texts from the Epistles, and texts from Revelation. Conrad is increasingly convinced that the Apocalypse is not at hand and increasingly disturbed by that defect in the scheme of creation.

Francis Ford Coppola's melodramatic retitling of *Heart of Darkness* to *Apocalypse Now* mistakes both literary and cultural history. Conrad's apocalypse is never "now," nor has it proved to be "now" for the modern world. The point in Conrad is always that the king does not come with a shout or even a whisper. Conrad reduces the Apocalypse to parody. That turn is in keeping with the time of *Under Western Eyes, Victory,* and *The Rescue,* the years just preceding and coincident with the years of the Great War that seemed as if it would never end.[1] The abiding pessimism of the war years affects Conrad's later work. *Victory* was revised and published, Conrad reminds us in the "notes" to the work of both 1915 and 1920, when the English and Germans alike were realizing that a "victory" could be but a hollow sham, *The Rescue* when everyone touched by the massacre knew that no "rescue" worth having could come to pass. A battlefield scene closes *Victory*, complete with corpses rotting in the sun and in the water. Jorgenson of *The Rescue*, the Norwegian of many languages who cannot remember his own, might stand for all Europeans, the dynamited *Emma* an image from the Western Front. The parodic irony that pervades Conrad's later work pervades the literature of the Great War. Conrad is one of its precursors. His secular apocalypse is ironic because it signifies nothing. Instead of endowing history with ultimate meaning, it signifies that history is meaningless.

But a historical explanation cannot finally satisfy. Conrad's later pessimism is actually more intense than that of the writers killed or made by the Great War. Despairing of transcendent meaning, the writers of the war characteristically performed immanent rescues of meaning, often through merely human relationships, through being in love. Except for Flora's ultimate union with Powell in *Chance*, a union hedged about with ironies, Conrad sedulously mines and destroys that surrogate for transcendence. Heyst cannot love Lena, and her love is a silly parody of divine love, leading to death by bullet, water, and fire. Edith Travers rejects Lingard. Rita, in *The Arrow of Gold*, abandons George after their alpine idyll. Conrad heaps coals of

---

[1] The following observations are indebted to Paul Fussell, *The Great War and Modern Memory*, pp. 3–35, 71–74, 114–44, 270–309.

scorn upon this poor substitute for transcendent significance. And with remarkable foresight he blasts the war writers' favorite surrogate for transcendence, homoerotic or homosexual love. The Anthony-Powell affair ("'I wasn't fit to tie the shoestrings of the man,'" Powell says [p. 440], and merrily marries his widow) burlesques homoerotic love, as the Ricardo-Jones liaison mocks homosexual love. What we find in later Conrad is certainly not shyness before the sexual shrine, as critics have traditionally alleged, but ridicule of sexual love as a meaningful surrogate for agape, for the promised king's wedding feast of the Apocalypse.

Conrad's nihilism goes beyond sex. Words and aesthetic form became another of the war writers' surrogates. Poets as unlike as Rosenberg and Owen, memorialists as unlike as Blunden and Graves found a defense against horror in the correct word and the formful narrative. They believed in the power of aesthetic structures to wrest meaning out of massacre. Conrad disbelieves. *Under Western Eyes, Chance, Victory,* and *The Rescue* reject the validity of aesthetic forms. They parody traditional structures and values. The "technique of disintegration" is the later Conrad's passion.[2] His "forms" imitate the Apocalypse.

Under Western Eyes is the still point, the place where Conrad begins to turn toward contempt and parody. We can designate exactly the scene in *Under Western Eyes* where Conrad turns his face to the wall.

The scene occurs early in part four, when the scapegrace Kostia comes to Razumov with the money he has stolen from his father, mournfully announcing the deed

[2]Northrop Frye, *Anatomy of Criticism*, p. 234.

with the simple words " 'It's done' " (p. 313). His words call
to Razumov's mind another scene, when he had waited in
his room for the moment of Haldin's arrest. Razumov then
is "reduced . . . to despair" because his watch has stopped.
He tries to dismiss his anxiety. " 'It's done,' " he says. " 'And
now to work.' " Visions of a lurking police agent disturb
his pathetic studies, and he tries to quell them with the
same simple phrase, "It is done." But immediately he realizes that it is not yet half-past twelve, so "It was not done,"
says the narrator, mimicking Razumov. Finally, when a
distant clock strikes one, he thinks (or the narrator records),
"This time it was done" (pp. 64–65). Here it is not possible
to distinguish Razumov from the elderly narrator. Ultimately, of course, this innocent phrase must be the translator's, reflecting his consciousness. What it reflects, again,
is his perdurable habit of seeing the world through the
English Bible. When he puts the same phrase in Kostia's
mouth, the context leaves no doubt about the perversity of
the narrator's typological imagination. When Razumov,
enjoying Kostia's moral seduction in another burlesque of
homoeroticism, persuades the young man to steal for him,
Kostia cries eagerly, " 'To the devil with the ten command-
ments. . . . It's the new future now.' " Kostia becomes an
enraptured visionary who sees the New Jerusalem coming
like a bride to the king's wedding, who sees "a new heaven
and a new earth" (Rev. 21:1–2; see also Isa. 66:22).[3] But

---

[3]"And I saw a new heaven and a new earth; for the first heaven
and the first earth were passed away; and there was no more sea"
(Rev. 21:1). Ford Madox Ford,"Decennial," *London Mercury* 32 (July,
1935):223, reports that Conrad "never tired of repeating Christine Rosetti's
last written words, 'A little while and we shall be there / Please God,
where there is no more sea.' "

when Kostia brings the stolen money, he is enraptured no
more:

"It's done," he said.

Razumov, sitting bowed, his clasped hands hanging between
his knees, shuddered at the familiar sound of the words. Kostia
deposited slowly in the circle of the lamplight a small brown par-
cel tied with a piece of string.

"As I've said—all I could lay my hands on. The old boy'll
think the end of the world has come." [P. 313]

The reader with an ear for Scripture may shudder delighted
at the familiar sound. Conrad parodies the climax of Revelation, when history imitates Razumov's watch and "'the
end of the world has come'":

Behold, I come as a thief. Blessed is he that watcheth and keepeth
his garments, lest he walk naked, and they see his shame. And
he gathered them together into a place called in the Hebrew
tongue Armageddon. And the seventh angel poured out his vial
into the air; and there came a great voice out of the temple of
heaven, from the throne, saying, It is done. [Rev. 16:15–17]

So Kostia comes as a thief, and the great voice of God becomes the scapegrace's slang.

This absurd mixture of text and context almost disinte-
grates the fiction. But *Under Western Eyes* remains this side
of traditional realism, for we can rationalize the absurd
mixture by saying that it shows that our translator is as
unreliable a narrator as English fiction affords.

Earlier I said that the professor detests Madame de S——
because she threatens his sense of identity rooted in the English Bible. But that explanation will not do. He puts the
perverted allusions to the promised land into her mouth,
just as he puts Revelation into Razumov's and into Kostia's.

His manic loathing for Madame de S——, then, is perhaps merely another sign of his instability, his unfitness to be our historian. Another is the resemblances he implies between himself and Razumov—a doubly erotic burlesque, projecting himself onto Razumov to realize his repressed desire for Natalia.[4] But the pervasive sign of the professor's unfitness is his devotion to the English Bible, and in particular to violent texts.

For example, he frames Razumov's encounter with Haldin with allusions to the parable of the king's wedding feast (Matt. 22:1-14; Luke 14:16-24). The king sends his servants to invite guests to the son's wedding, but the guests decline. When the king sends his servants a second time, a "remnant" of the invited guests beat and slay the messengers. After punishing the murderers, the king instructs his servants to "go out into the highways and hedges" to furnish the feast with guests (Luke 14:23). Matthew adds the unfortunate compelled guest without a wedding garment (cf. Rev. 16:15) who is "cast . . . into outer darkness" where "there shall be weeping and gnashing of teeth" (Matt. 22:13). Haldin alludes to the parable when he describes " 'the sound of weeping and gnashing of teeth [de P——] raised in the land' " (p. 16), and again when Razumov returns from Ziemianitch's stable, saying of the sledge driver that " 'the guests for the feast of freedom must be sought in byways and hedges' " (p. 56). So the allusions neatly frame Razumov's going and coming back. But the Professor's rendition of the parable is nearly as absurd as his transformation of Kostia. God the King sending his apostolic servants to preach the gospel of redemption first to Israel and then more forcibly

---

[4]On these resemblances see Claire Rosenfield, *Paradise of Snakes: An Archetypal Analysis of Conrad's Political Novels*, pp. 161-66.

114

to the Gentiles becomes Haldin sending Razumov to Zie-mianitch, who, like the first guests, does not come. Revers-ing the fate of the scriptural messengers, Razumov thrashes the invited guest. The Gentiles become the next batch of guests Razumov invites, his father and General T——, who thrash the king. Even more bizarre, the initial allusion makes de P—— into the King of the Last Judgment, send-ing the unredeemed to the "outer darkness" of hell. The professor's metaphors are so egregiously mixed that they become those "vaticinations" rendering Scripture and the Christian virtues indecent.

Another sign of the professor's typological fixation is the disposition of Scriptures in *Under Western Eyes*. They are thickest, thirteen, in part 1, the only part in which the professor does nothing but "translate" Razumov's docu-ment. Part 2, describing the professor's relation with the Haldins, Natalia's chateau visit, her first glimpse of Razu-mov, and the conversation between Razumov and the Pro-fessor, contains only five allusions. They are thick again in part 3—eleven—where again the translator relies on Razumov's record to describe Razumov's interviews with Peter Ivanovitch and Madame de S——, Tekla, and Sophia Antonovna, ending with Razumov by the effigy of Rousseau writing his first report to Councillor Mikulin. They are thinnest, two, in part 4; although its first section, the flash-back (pp. 293–316), confines the Professor to his document again, and to Revelation, he participates in the remainder of the action. Thus when the professor is outside his direct experience, scriptural texts flourish. When he is involved in the action, allusions fade, and those that do appear tend to be obvious protrusions—Rachel's mourning, Judas, the Samaritan—rather than intertwined with dialogue and ac-tion. The disposition of scriptures, then, suggests that the professor seizes desperately upon the English Bible to settle his strange country with images he understands. But this way of seeing fails.

The novel's first allusion quietly forewarns us not to trust in the Professor's eyes. After disqualifying himself to tell his tale by announcing that he has "no comprehension of the Russian character," the professor remarks that "it would be idle to inquire why Mr. Razumov has left this record behind him. It is inconceivable that he would have wished any human eye to see it" (pp. 4–5). Yet writing well after Razumov has delivered himself into the hands of his enemies and after the more tender hands of Tekla have recovered him, the professor knows that Razumov did indeed want Natalia's eye to see his record. What the professor means is that the wish is "inconceivable" to him. Nonetheless, he proceeds to give the first of his several idle inquiries into Razumov's motive for leaving his document, conceiving the inconceivable through the dark glass of Scripture:

Being myself a quiet individual I take it that all men are really after is some form or perhaps only some formula of peace. Certainly they are crying loud enough for it at the present day. What sort of peace Kirylo Sidorovitch Razumov expected to find in the writing up of his record it passeth my understanding to guess. [P. 5]

The professor seems to distinguish between the substance of "peace," the thing itself, and its "form" or "formula." Because the thing in itself is beyond our apprehension or our grasp, we must be satisfied with its appearances or with phrases that signify it. His allusion conveys both form and formula: "The peace of God which passeth all understanding . . ." (Phil. 4:7). Paul specifically tells the Philippians that a loving Christian community is one that imitates

Christ, that it must be made in his image even as he is "in the form of God" (2:4-6). But the professor does not allude only to Philippians. He alludes also to the Book of Common Prayer. Conrad's Anglican readers in 1911 would have recognized his allusion instantly and perhaps thought no more about it, because it introduces the Blessing that concludes the Order for Holy Communion:

The Peace of God, which passeth all understanding, keep your minds and hearts in the knowledge and love of God, and of his Son Jesus Christ Our Lord: And the Blessing of God Almighty, the Father, the Son, and the Holy Ghost, be amongst you, and remain with you always.

This is the professor's formula. He alludes, then, perhaps less to Paul than to the Church of England. The allusion is less Pauline than English, less spiritual than cultural. The professor again invokes "form" against the "inconceivable" politics of Natalia's *mouvements d'âme* when he declares to her: "'Life is a thing of form. It has its plastic shape and definite intellectual aspect. The most idealistic conceptions of love and forbearance must be clothed in flesh as it were before they can be made understandable'" (p. 106). So the Word becomes flesh and dwells among the professor of languages. He clothes the politics and passions of inchoate Russian mysticism with the decent black broadcloth of the English Bible, a formful and formulaic Anglicanism his tailor.

The professor's translation is thoroughly tainted by his Anglican eyes, and we cannot see except through them. James's image for *Chance*, subjective hovering, would do admirably to describe the perspective of *Under Western Eyes.* Conrad begins to disintegrate realistic assumptions. Characters, events, and actions are not meaningful in any traditional mimetic sense. *Under Western Eyes* is not about a young man's fall and redemption. That comfortable formula will not do. The subject of *Under Western Eyes* is precisely what the title says, alien perceptions. All we can know is a typological imagination hovering above the end of things, what the seventh angel sees.

The allegory of the king's wedding has a long and typical history in Conrad. "The destiny of this nation is to be accomplished in darkness amidst much weeping and gnashing of teeth," Conrad writes to Spiridion Kliszczewski (December 19, 1885) about the fate of England.[5] He twice uses the image in early letters to his aunt.[6] It does not enter fiction until "The End of the Tether" (p. 324), not to reappear until *Under Western Eyes*. *Chance* (p. 172) and *The Rescue* (pp. 151, 385) use it also. The pattern is usual, references concentrated in early letters and late fiction. Letters seem to have been Conrad's proving ground for scriptural rhetoric. Allusions come thick in letters until 1910, then fade dramatically. But then they flourish in the fiction. The pattern argues Conrad's conscious habituation to scriptural rhetoric.

This pattern does not hold, however, for references to the great voice of God and to Revelation as a whole. The last book of the New Testament fascinates Conrad, and not always for its parodic potentialities. For example, it is on Conrad's mind when he recalls his father's funeral in "Poland Revisited": "There was nothing in my aching head but a few words, some such stupid sentences as, 'It's done,' or 'It's accomplished' (in Polish it is much shorter), or something of the sort, repeating itself endlessly" (*Notes*, p. 169).

[5] G. Jean-Aubry, *Joseph Conrad: Life and Letters*, 1:84.
[6] Joseph Conrad, *Letters of Joseph Conrad to Marguerite Poradowska, 1890–1920*, ed. and trans. John A. Gee and Paul J. Sturm, pp. 36, 91.

It is hard to imagine a locution "much shorter" than two syllables, and the adjective qualifies seriousness, too. But the facile ironies cannot conceal how potent was Conrad's memory of his father—omnipotent in metaphor.

Perhaps the parodies of the great voice in *Under Western Eyes* and *The Rescue* are attempts to quiet that father's voice. But there are several allusions to Revelation in the early fiction too, most notably in *Nostromo*. Nostromo's "'Like a thief'" (p. 540) may echo Revelation as well as the Sermon on the Mount, a metaphor for his world's end. Giselle evidently stimulates the simile when she, elevating Nostromo to "'master'" of her "'soul,'" cries out, "'but it is done'" (p. 539). Her language prefigures Winnie's to Comrade Ossipon, Lena's to Heyst. The erotic encounter is not an effective surrogate for revelation. Neither is suicide. Although the sound of a fallen scull strikes Decoud's ears like "a revelation" when he rows out to shoot and drown the body of this death, though his last words are, "'It is done,'" no revelatory knowledge is given him. Instead Decoud is "swallowed up in the immense indifference of things" (pp. 500–501). The stark contrast with the message of the body of Hirsch's death, "a signal in the night," further emphasizes Decoud's vacuity.

Once again these echoes have the spontaneous, unstudied appearance typical of the early fiction. Mixed metaphors, not parodies, the allusions characterize the egoism that Hirsch transcends but Decoud and Nostromo cannot. The echoes of the world's end when we shall put off this body and be changed deride their vanity. Scripture retains its normative value. That is not the case in *Under Western Eyes,* where the studied allusion mocks at seeing by way of Scripture. Nor is it the case in *Victory,* which takes its title and its theme from what Conrad calls, in "The Life

Beyond," the "tinkling cymbals book" (*Notes*, p. 68), Paul's
First Epistle to the Corinthians.

To hearten the Corinthians, Paul vouchsafes them a vision
of the resurrection of the dead:

Behold, I shew you a mystery; We shall not all sleep, but we shall
all be changed, In a moment, in the twinkling of an eye, at the
last trump; for the trumpet shall sound, and the dead shall be
raised incorruptible, and we shall be changed. For this corruptible
must put on incorruption, and this mortal must put on immortality. So when this corruptible shall have put on incorruption,
and this mortal shall have put on immortality, then shall be
brought to pass the saying that is written, Death is swallowed
up in victory. O death, where is thy sting? O grave, where is
thy victory? The sting of death is sin; and the strength of sin
is the law. But thanks be to God, which giveth us the victory
through our Lord Jesus Christ. [1 Cor. 15:51–57]

Paul's text is the core of *Victory*, or its sting. That the work
contains many biblical allusions has been known for some
time. Wilfred Dowden has given us the fullest account of
them, including two to 1 Corinthians: when Heyst, with
witting irony, tells Lena that "'hope is a Christian virtue'"
(p. 355), Conrad expects us to hear the last verse of the great
hymn to love (13:13); when Heyst muses, "'There must be
a lot of the original Adam in me, after all'" (p. 173), he
alludes, now probably unwittingly, to Paul's doctrine of the
old Adam and the new (15:45–50) rather than to Genesis.
Using these observations and others, Dowden then plausibly
explains "the ambiguity of the title" through Heyst's role
as an ironic Christ.[7] But Dowden misses the allusion in

[7] Wilfred P. Dowden, *Joseph Conrad: The Imaged Style*, pp. 156–66.

the title, the parodic metaphor that says that the title is not ambiguous at all. I am not about to rest my case on the repetition of a single noun. A trail of allusions to Paul's vision of the Lord's Day runs throughout *Victory*. Its import is depressing evidence of the depth of the vale of despair that swallowed up Conrad in the last ten years of his life. The trail begins with Jones's "devilish" and "waspish" eyebrows (pp. 115, 341), which suggest "the will and power to sting—something vicious, unconquerable, and deadly" (p. 384). We may be certain that Conrad has Paul's question to Death in mind. He had evidently been rereading 1 Corinthians while he was writing *Victory* and found that Paul's question deserves an answer. At a child's funeral the young captain of "A Smile of Fortune" remembers reading Paul's "words of hope and defiance" at sea burials but asks now on the pathetic occasion, " 'What was the use of asking Death where her sting was . . . ?' " (p. 16). The captain's feminine pronoun says a great deal about why he cannot manage Alice Jacobus. Conrad replies directly to Paul in his "Titanic Inquiry," now using the neuter pronoun, saying of the victims of that disaster, "Death has its sting" (*Notes*, p. 247). Jones, then, is Paul's death, the sting of spiritual death, with the crucial difference that Conrad's death is "unconquerable." This "spectre . . . from Hades," this "starved spectre" with "a death's head grin," this "merry skeleton" (pp. 116, 118, 230, 319) represents the "spiritual starvation" that the good Davidson feared would visit Heyst on Samburan. Indeed, just before the dehydrated Jones and his companions make Samburan, we are treated to Marlow's mad metaphor in *Chance*. To Lena, we are told, the sea was "the abomination of desolation" (p. 199)—now, though, in Matthew's sense, a sign that an age of "false Christs" will begin (Matt. 24:15, 24).[8] But Conrad's anti-Christ cannot be "swallowed up in victory," only, like Decoud, "swallowed up in the immense indifference of things," of Conrad's moral imagination.

Paul's verses resound like a mocking echo when Lena disarms Ricardo, receives the bullet meant for him, and dies wrapped in the illusion of her "victory." For Lena mistakes physical for spiritual death. Ricardo seems to stand for physical death, "a best of prey" prone to "straightforward violence" who must "ravish or kill" (pp. 288, 292, 293). But Lena mistakes him for "the embodied evil of the world" and imagines that evil distilled in his knife (p. 298). As she waits for the man "of violence and death" on the night of her own, the narrator describes her secret purpose "of capturing death—savage, sudden, irresponsible death, . . . death embodied in the knife" (p. 394). This is Lena's way of thinking, not the narrator's or Conrad's. She has constructed an allegorical fantasy in which she stars. Thus when she extracts Ricardo's knife, she thinks that she has "the very sting of death in her hands." She thinks she holds Paul's "sin," the knife a weapon that "seemed to have drawn into itself every danger and menace of the death-ridden earth" (p. 399). Like Jones and like Heyst, Lena is a parody of Christ.

At this point Ricardo incongruously cries out, as if partaking in her fantasy, "'You forgave me. You saved me'" (pp. 399–400). Conrad's parody is savage. Lena imagines that she has the power of Christ, the power to "carry off the terrible spoil, the sting of vanquished death" (p. 401). But Lena dies instead. The echoes of Paul mock her even as she dies, "as if fatigued only by the exertions of her tre-

<hr/>

[8]The allusion appears a third time in The Arrow of Gold. After a night's bad sleep brought on by his interview with Madame Blunt, George calls his nightmares "the abomination of desolation to me" (p. 154).

mendous victory, capturing the very sting of death in the service of love" (p. 405). The context raises the Christ parody several decibels, for, unlike Christ, Lena does not choose death; she does not even know that she is dying for love, for the want of it. At her dying, "convinced of the reality of her victory over death," Conrad trebles the violent mixture of metaphors by making Lena allude to Paul, to Revelation (21:4), and perhaps to Donne's Holy Sonnet 10, itself built upon both biblical texts: "'No more,' she muttered. 'There will be no more! Oh, my beloved,' she cried weakly, 'I've saved you.'" But the point is that Lena cannot save. When, finally, she asks Heyst, "'Who else could have done this for you?,'" he replies with charming accuracy, "'No one in the world'" (p. 406). There is no Christ in Heyst's wasteland, and no authentic, saving imitation of Christ in Conrad. Those who attempt it have his genial contempt. *Victory* inverts allegory. There will be more death. Jones shoots Ricardo; Wang shoots Pedro; Jones commits suicide. Heyst burns himself and Lena's remains. Conrad leaves us with the book's last word, "'Nothing'"

But that last word is less instructive about the novel's dominant idea than its two beginnings, Conrad's notes. One of the reasons that critics have wrestled with the title of *Victory* is that Conrad clouds the issue—deliberately, I suspect—in his note to the first edition. There he says that the title was the last word of the novel he wrote and implies that he wrote it in a gust of "pagan" inspiration (p. vii). Although concerned that the title might leave him open to the charge of commercialism, Conrad tells us that he let it stand as an omen that England would triumph against its enemies in the Great War. This first gloss, then, gives the title hopeful, positive connotations. Conrad feigns confessional openness with intent to deceive. The war done, however, Conrad is more candid in the note of the edition of 1920, even indirectly hinting at the title's source and giving us a reading of the novel's dominant idea with an accuracy that criticism has not surpassed. Again Conrad is apologetic. He confesses to feeling uneasy that his "bit of imagined drama" should have appeared in an apocalyptic time, "in the crash of the big guns and in the din of brave words expressing the truth of an indomitable faith" (p. ix). The concatenating diction reveals, I think, not irony but sarcasm: the "faith," Conrad implies, is neither indomitable nor true. Nor is Conrad commending humankind when he opines that publication in time of war did not matter because man will endure the apocalypse, that man will go on reading even if "the trump of the Last Judgment [were] to sound suddenly." Are we, he asks, "to let ourselves be disturbed by an angel's vengeful music too mighty for our ears and too awful for our terrors?" (p. ix). The allusion foreshadows the rhetoric of Conrad's allusions in *Victory*, denying Paul's indomitable faith that "we shall all be changed, In a moment, in the twinkling of an eye, at the last trump; for the last trumpet shall sound, and the dead shall be changed incorruptible, and we shall all be changed." Conrad insists that we shall not be changed, that the pianist will continue playing Beethoven and the cobbler will "stick to his last," that "the reader will go on reading if the book pleases him and the critic will go on criticizing with that faculty of detachment born perhaps from a sense of infinite littleness and which is yet the only faculty that seems to assimilate man to the immortal gods" (p. x).

Conrad's notion of endurance seems a world apart from Faulkner's. Conrad's is a parody of humanism. We will endure not because we are decent or because we are adaptable beasts or because we have the stuff of heroism in us—

Homeric or Pauline—but because we are infinitely little. That is the dominant idea of *Victory*, "infinite littleness," the triviality of mankind and of the gods. The title is not serious or tragic. It is not ironic or ambiguous. It is savage parody, a despairing sneer. *Victory* has had a contentious critical history. Esteemed by an early generation of Conradians, the novel was then savaged in later critiques, of which Thomas Moser's is the most thorough and perceptive, though marred by a host of silent assumptions about novels.[9] After Moser, attempts to rehabilitate *Victory* have usually proceeded by refuting his charge of aesthetic incompetence. Sharon Kahele and Howard German, for example, argue for the work's integrity as a realistic action, while John Palmer has shown us better than anyone else how dazzlingly complex are the various strands of imagery in *Victory*.[10] My commentary would seem to support claims for aesthetic competence. But if *Victory* is a brilliant "bit of imagined drama," it is a loathly brilliance. Moser may be mistaken about the novel's technical incompetence, but about its moral incompetence—its deathly pessimism, its contempt—Moser is surely correct.

Except that he does not go far enough. Moser holds that in *Victory*, and in other late works, Conrad's "intended meaning is at variance with the actual meaning" or "deeper impulses." Specifically, Moser feels that Conrad meant to exalt the saving power of romantic love but failed because he disbelieved his theme. Thus, of the end-

[9]Thomas Moser, *Joseph Conrad: Achievement and Decline*, pp.102–63. See Moser's review of the more enthusiastic studies preceding his own, pp. 131–32.

[10]Sharon Kahele and Howard German, "Conrad's *Victory*: A Reassessment," *MFS* 10 (Spring, 1964):55–72; John A. Palmer, *Joseph Conrad: A Study in Literary Growth*, pp. 166–97.

ing of *Victory*, Moser writes, "The inner Conrad, incorrigibly denying his conscious intention that Heyst is to be saved through his love for Lena, effectively demonstrates his disbelief in the resolution of the theme by making the resolution of the plot utterly incredible."[11] The reading I have given is much bleaker than Moser's: the ending is the inevitable outcome of Conrad's conscious intentions. One of the reasons that we have so much incidental and extended criticism rooting out allusions is that their presence gauges conscious intention, especially when we deal with reiterated verbal allusions. Conrad's references to "victory" and "the sting of death" are too frequent and too precise to be due to chance alone or to unconscious design. These allusions comprise the controlling parodic metaphor of *Victory*, a metaphor that breaks up the realistic structure of the novel and declares that Conrad's conscious intentions perfectly match his deeper impulses. Lena's accidental death, Heyst's melodramatic end, the mechanical murders of Pedro and Ricardo, and Jones's melodramatic end all say that life is cheap. Conrad never intends, on either the surface or the deeper levels of his book, to have Heyst "saved through his love for Lena." Indeed, allusions aside, what evidence is there that we are supposed to believe that Heyst loves? The surface evidence is all the other way. Conrad's conscious intent and deep impulse are to show that human love is impossible (Heyst) or ineffectual (Lena) and that human evil is ineffectual (Ricardo) or ridiculous (Jones) in a world that prizes coal above diamonds, a world where even Judgment Day would not arouse us from our daily round. In such a world a love like Lena's becomes a futile, grotesque caricature of re-

---

[11] Moser, *Joseph Conrad*, p. 109.

demption. "'No one in the world'" could redeem Axel Heyst. And no one in the world can be redeemed. We are too little to be worth redemption.

Even if the realistic criteria such as credibility and plausibility are inapplicable to *Victory,* criteria from other venerable and still admired rhetorical traditions could be applied to show its aesthetic failings. Quintilian, thinking of Socrates and Plato, would, of course, deny that I can separate the beautiful and the good. If, in *Victory,* Conrad is a bad man speaking well, then *Victory* is ugly.

Generic theory might also be applied. Moser's realistic perspective is neither naïve nor inexplicable. The first part of *Victory* gives out many signals to the reader that he has a realistic fiction, a novel, in hand. The historical observation of the first paragraph, the specific setting of the action in place and time (the Dent edition even provides a map of the locale), the characterizations of Heyst and Schomberg, Schomberg's employment, and Heyst's biography all smack of realism. A louder signal than any of these is the mechanism of the frame narrative that Conrad takes pains to start up and then abandons after one hundred pages. Albert Guerard, following Moser's novelistic evaluation, singles out this narrative inconsistency as a telling sign of the work's aesthetic failure.[12] But the argument that Conrad abandoned the frame mechanism out of weariness or inattention does not convince me. Would it not be more reasonable to assume, given the history of Conrad's uses of the frame mechanism, that he drops it deliberately? In the early fiction, *Youth, Heart of Darkness,* and *Lord Jim,* Conrad uses the frame mechanism for realism's sake, to impart a sense of

[12] Albert Guerard, *Conrad the Novelist,* pp. 273–74.

historical authenticity, but not in his later work. In *Under Western Eyes* the elderly professor, presumably under the constraints of his own experience and Razumov's diary, can have no possible source for portions of his narrative. Nor can Marlow in *Chance*, who adds to those implausibilities his own wild speculations about facts, acts, and motives. The narrative implausibility of *Victory* is far more flagrant: Conrad sets his mechanism humming and then walks away. Given this history, I doubt that Conrad simply botched his job in *Victory*. He drops the frame on purpose. The opening frame perspective and other signals of realism are meant, I suspect, to lead us on. Conrad sets up expectations so that he can frustrate them. The title's sneer is meant for the reader too. We expect one kind of fiction, a novel, and get another.

But what other? John Palmer struggles to find an apt name for the genre to which *Victory* belongs. Following ample precedents, first he calls it "allegorical or near-allegorical," then "semiallegorical symbology," next "an allegorical narrative," and finally claims that it has a "consistent tone of Christian allegory."[13] Despite his gradually more assertive stance, Palmer's first two attempts suggest that he is uneasy with the idea of *Victory* as allegory, and with good reason. Frye distinguishes between formal and naïve allegory and suggests that we call a work a formal allegory only when it has three essential characteristics, and then only "cautiously": it is a "structure of images, not of disguised ideas," images coherent apart from their ideas; it assumes and demonstrates "a continuous relationship between art and nature," continuously and consistently indicating "the relationship of [its] im-

---

[13] Palmer, *Joseph Conrad*, pp. 168, 169, 173, 188.

ages to examples and precepts"; most vital, the writer must "explicitly" indicate that relationship, clearly saying, "'By this I also *(allos)* mean that.'"[14] On the last test alone, *Victory* falls out from the ranks of allegories. It fails the second test, too. But if Palmer and a half-dozen other readers have resorted to "allegory" as a way to explain the structure of *Victory,* the impulse is understandable. Just as Conrad leads us to expect a novel, he seduces us into allegory—chiefly through his scriptures but also through animal imagery and certain "semiallegorical" symbols, such as Heyst's neighboring volcano, the person of "plain Mr. Jones," and Ricardo's knife. But the reader who tries to pin these images to precepts will fail, if "moral precepts" means a coherent, consistent set of ideas that will guide us through the dark wood or up the winding stair. A writer convinced of littleness human and divine does not proffer precepts.

Victory is neither novel nor allegory. The ranks of satire might take it in, since *Victory* ridicules Christian eschatology, the sentimentalism of a reading public, critical expectations, and the humanist tradition. But satire works by invoking positive values antithetical to the surface narrative. Satire has an object. *Victory* does not. The work is all subject—overwhelmingly negative, relentlessly parodic, its contempt so great that it rejects the validity of aesthetic structures.

Victory illustrates the limits of scriptural rhetoric. For although Moser is certainly mistaken in his specific formulation, *Victory* evidently fails to realize one of Conrad's conscious intentions. The work is Conrad's last try

---

[14] Frye, *Anatomy of Criticism,* pp. 90–91.

at a problem that had always intrigued him, depicting deviant religious experience. Comparison of the manuscript of *Victory* with the printed version, in particular his revisions of the biblical allusions, revisions of characterization, and the history of the last chapter, suggests that Conrad wanted to treat of deviant spiritual experience but found that he could not manage the personalities and motives of people in the grip of religious crisis. Failing that, he relies overmuch upon scriptural rhetoric to carry the burden. Hence the theme becomes unconvincing, vague, and confused.

I have already remarked some changes in the biblical allusions from manuscript to novel, that they are revised to become more specific. This is characteristic of all of the revisions of scriptural texts in *Victory*, including the titular allusions. The manuscript rendition of Jones's eyebrows, where the trail begins, reads, "Only his thin beautifully pencilled eyebrows drawn together a little suggested the will and power to sting—something vicious unconquered and deadly" (MS, pp. 1081–82).[15] The novel adds the adjective "waspish" and alters "unconquered" to the more ominous "unconquerable" (p. 384). Slight changes, but meant to vivify the description so that we will hear the echo of Paul's rhetorical question, "O death, where is thy sting?" But Conrad worries about his readers who are hard of hearing. The next altered passage occurs when Lena has captured Ricardo's knife. Here the manuscript gives "The forest! The forest! were the two words ringing in her head louder and louder, more commanding every second" (MS, p. 1118). Revising, Conrad includes Paul's

---

[15] In the Humanities Research Center, University of Texas at Austin. The abbreviation MS in parentheses signifies manuscript pagination.

question again: "Yes, the forest—that was the place for her
to carry off the terrible spoil, the sting of vanquished death"
(pp. 400-401). When next we hear Paul, Lena is dying after
"capturing the very sting of death in the service of love"
(p. 405), where the only change from the manuscript is
"love" for "life" (MS, p. 1126). The change signifies the
love Paul celebrates (1 Cor. 13), and that Lena, in her fantasy, is Christian love. Finally, the last allusion to Paul
in the final version mutes the message by extracting au-
thorial commentary from the manuscript. As Heyst and
Davidson watch ineffectually, "The spirit of the girl which
was passing away from under them clung to her triumph
convinced of the reality of her victory over death" (p. 406).
The manuscript calls her spirit "naïve and convinced,"
and it adds a phrase, "death stalking about the world"
(MS, p. 1127). The deletions dim the irony at the cost of
placing all the burden of its meaning on the mixed metaphor created by the clash of fictionalized and scriptural
contexts. The essential problem, however, is not with perceiving the Scripture but with Conrad's failure to dramatize Lena's delusion.

Ian Watt, pointing out peculiarities in the way Conrad
names his characters, surmises that the act was crucial
for Conrad because the names he chose were often "a symbolic token . . . of his own personal identity."[16] The manuscript of *Victory* shows Conrad struggling to name and
characterize his principals, especially Lena and Heyst. Perhaps he struggles because genuine religious crisis was not
a part "of his own personal identity."

Revising Jones from manuscript to novel, Conrad re-

[16]Ian Watt, "*Almayer's Folly*: Memories and Models," *Mosaic* 8 (Fall,
1974):169-70.

duces his deviant priestliness and magnifies the demonic. With his complement, Lena, the balance tilts in the same way. The changes from manuscript to final form show Conrad muting her saintliness and finally finding the ambiguity he wants in an allusion rather than in a dramatic rendering. The business of Lena's triple naming is heavy in the manuscript, and Conrad experiments, apparently listening for the correct symbolic note to sound. The first effort at a name occurs when it does in the final version. Heyst has known her for several days when it occurs to him that he does not know her name. She replies, "'They have named me Alma. I don't know why. Silly name. Margaret, too'" (MS, p. 223). She is "Margaret" again when Heyst next sees her (MS, p. 235), a passage deleted from the novel. Conrad next attempts "Madelaine," and now he has Heyst's name for her: "The girl they had called Alma (she did not know why) Madelaine too—and whom he called Lena" (MS, p. 606). Finally, in another passage excised from the novel, Conrad finds the name he wants. Lena interrupts Heyst reading about "'the misfortune of mankind'": "Lena's voice spoke above his drooping head, the voice of the girl they had called Alma (she didn't know why also Magdalen)" (MS, p. 617; cf. *Victory*, p. 220). Here the g is heavily inked over another letter, possibly *d*, as if Conrad had begun to write "Madelaine" when he heard the note for which he had been listening. "Magdalene" she becomes for the rest of the manuscript, and the allusion appears more often there than in the novel.

The first of Conrad's tries, Margaret, suggests that he may indeed have had in mind Goethe's *Faust* as an analogue for the plot of *Victory*, a thesis developed by Alice

Raphael.[17] Abandoning "Margaret," however, may indicate that Conrad thought the analogue could not or should not be sustained, as it is not in novel or manuscript. Faust's Margaret is all saint. "Madelaine," on the other hand, is too Proustian. "Magdalene" gets the ambiguity—by tradition, though without scriptural warrant, the prostitute Jesus saves from stoning. Conrad may also have wanted us to recall the woman whom John contrasts with doubting Thomas (20:1–31), our Heyst. But even if the note is right, it is awfully loud, especially combined with the insistent "Alma," considering that Conrad revises elsewhere toward implication. It trumpets spiritual ambiguity perhaps because Conrad could not render the theme into credible action.

Yet Conrad tries to mute other displays of Lena's spirituality in the transition from manuscript to novel. The manuscript Lena is a "sacred" Cockney girl who loves Heyst because she "admired the genius for kindliness which she saw shining in him with an exceptional splendour of perfection" (MS, pp. 186, 192, 237–38). There is more in the manuscript about her enthralling voice, the evanescent physical trait which "seduces" Heyst, finding "its way into [his] heart" (MS, p. 192). The manuscript Lena wants Heyst's soul joined to her own. At the turning point of the plot Conrad tells us explicitly that Lena is motivated by spiritual lust. Lena has decided to keep Heyst innocent of Ricardo's attack and to fight the coming battle by herself:

. . . she would have used incantations or philtres without hesitation. For joined to her greed of a personal triumph, there was

[17] Alice Raphael, *Goethe the Challenger*, pp. 39–83.

in her an admiring [?] distrust of the man. He seemed to her too good. . . . Without knowing it she had transported this situation in a spiritual region where she would fight not for his life but for his admired, loved, incomprehensible, infinitely precious identity—to save it, to penetrate it, to mingle with it—to make it her own. [MS, p. 893; cf. *Victory*, p. 317]

This deleted passage specifies what Conrad intended by Lena's "victory." She wages her battle not in desiccated Samburan but in a transsubstantial realm. Her fight is metaphysical. Conrad here sets the task his revisions try to accomplish. He wants to show Lena unwittingly in the grip of metaphysical desire, "without knowing it." It is an ambitious project. To do it well means a dramatic rendering of spiritual conflict and clear signals that the narrator does not share Lena's delusion. Instead, Conrad relies on "Magdalene" and other allusions. In the finished novel the narrator seems to share Lena's delusion, and neither manuscript nor novel successfully dramatizes the terms of Lena's conflict. They barely dramatize them at all.

Why is this individual ripe to be bitten by erotic religiosity? The only clues Conrad offers are that people have been too many for Lena all of her days, Heyst's generosity flatters her, and she remembers her Sunday-school lessons. Because Lena's spiritual conflict is so vaguely depicted in the novel, her scheme to steal Ricardo's knife seems incredibly fatuous. Fatuity of some kind can be credible enough under stress, but Lena's is beyond the patience of many readers. The fault lies in Conrad's inability to render the psychology of a good and simple person in thrall to a religious delusion. Without that, her obsession with the knife must seem fatuous and fair game for readers of a Freudian cast. The manuscript, then, shows how much Lena troubled Conrad. Neither there nor in the novel is she consistent, whether we measure by the norms of realism or by the norms of romance. Conrad was equally troubled by Axel Heyst. The trouble begins with his name. As is well known, Heyst was originally christened Augustus Berg. What is less well known is that he remains Berg until the last ten pages of the manuscript. That is a radical departure from Conrad's usual process of invention. Usually he begins with his protagonist's name, and that name is his working title. Thus *Under Western Eyes* was "Razumov"; *The Secret Agent* was "Verloc"; *The Rescue* for years was "Rescuer"; *Lord Jim* was "Jim"; *Nostromo* was always "Nostromo." Conrad seldom seems to have had a plot in mind when he began to write, often not knowing whether he was beginning a short story, a novella, or a novel. Thus he had often to revise furiously. Revisions to a final version do not, however, involve marked changes in the personality of a protagonist. It was otherwise with *Victory*, indicating how unsure Conrad was of Axel Heyst. First he is Augustus Berg, then Axel Berg, then A. C. Berg, and after that merely Berg, until he is suddenly transformed into Heyst (MS, p. 1130). The manuscript offers not the least clue about Conrad's motives, but they must have been compelling, because Conrad gave up several fine touches for "Heyst." For one, the change deemphasizes the analogy with Villier's Axël, whose protagonist is surnamed Auersperg,[18] as it deemphasizes the doubling with Schomberg. It meant surrendering some telling word plays—"'I'll drift,' Berg said," for example (MS, p. 234; cf. *Victory*, p. 92)—and an extensive image pattern juxtaposing Berg and the volcano, much more active in the manuscript, as is Berg.

[18]Jocelyn Baines, *Joseph Conrad: A Critical Biography*, p. 399.

Heyst of the novel is Paul's lukewarm man; Berg is fre-
netic, blowing hot and cold, a trait the name Augustus
Berg suggests. It is not, for example, Morrison but Berg
who urges the coal business and sends Morrison back to
England for its sake. Hence his retreat to Samburan after
Morrison dies makes sense, for Berg is to blame (MS, pp.
52–55, 171). Later in the manuscript Conrad reworks references to their coal business as they stand in the novel.
But, from carelessness perhaps, he leaves an inconsistency.
How can one reconcile Lena's Heyst with Hard Facts Heyst,
advocate of "'the stride forward'" (Victory, pp. 6–7)? Conrad failed to remove all traces of the hot Augustus Berg.

He did, however, carefully remove the icier traits,
letting them live only by implication. Berg's eremitic
penchant is one. There is much more in the manuscript
about Berg's failing a hermit's vocation, since the failure
is more radical in the manuscript (MS, pp. 80–84, 631–35).
There is also considerable stress on Berg's virginity. He
is, says Davidson, "'just a blessed innocent'" (MS, p. 160),
and Davidson expatiates at length about this pure and
holy Berg. Therefore, the physical sensations Lena gives
astound Berg and confound him because "he had known
no women" (MS, pp. 581–83, 595–96). Their sexual relationship is more specific, though nothing to annoy a cen-
sor. Sex disappoints A. C. Berg. His "moments of passion"
with Lena do not transform them into the yolk and white
of the one shell. For Berg had had "some unconscious
dream of rare and unique perfection" (MS, p. 596), a fit-
ting echo of Lena's thought about Berg's perfection and of
her equally unconscious transportation of their affair to
the realm of the spirits. The wreck of Berg's dream prompts
him to regret rescuing Lena "in a moment of emotional
folly" (MS, p. 596). All of these reflections occur when

Heyst-Berg is upset by Lena's half belief in Schomberg's calumny. The manuscript makes his motivation more complex: Lena's half belief upsets Berg because it proves that sexual love has not opened the way to metaphysical fulfillment. Of this the novel gives the barest hint, but with the reverse implication. Heyst's anger cools when he recalls that Lena "had a special grace in the intimacy of life." She "excites—and escapes" (*Victory*, p. 215). There follows immediately the sexual embrace that the novel suggests by the white space between chapters (*Victory*, pp. 215-16) and the manuscript treats a bit more boldly, concentrating on the striking detail that Lena cries the while. But Berg's metaphysical lust is frustrated: he feels "no nearer to his possession" (MS, p. 598). In the final Heyst there is little sign of the man whom sexual love confounds and dissatisfies. Conrad revised toward a lukewarm sexual stereotype without frustrated dreams of attaining spiritual perfection through the flesh. If traces of the hot Berg remained, the cold Berg of spiritual yearnings vanished.

Except, perhaps, for the name *Heyst*. It has been suggested that Conrad found a rhyme for Christ.[19] A chime with *iced* and *highest* might have attracted, too, as well as a pun on *heist*. Conrad did, in fact, write to his agent, Pinker (October 10, 1913), that he was searching for a name with a proper sound: "*Berg* won't do and I haven't been able as yet to find another name of the proper sonority."[20] If Conrad intended rhyming sonorities, the re-

[19]Bernard C. Meyer, *Joseph Conrad: A Psychoanalytic Biography*, p. 352.

[20]As quoted in Frederick R. Karl, *Joseph Conrad: The Three Lives*, p. 739. I have been told that the normal Swedish pronunciation would be "Hayst," which puns neatly with "Axel."

vision would be of a piece with "Magdalene," trying to evoke spiritual crisis by a name. I would not quarrel with Conrad's decision against some of the vacillations of Berg. Berg's forty-year-old virginity and his dream of metaphysical satisfaction through the flesh are jejune traits in which no one could honestly believe. Evidently Conrad could not. Yet he wants the spiritual conflict that he is unable to represent. So he tries to resume the conflict in a name. A name is not enough.

Nor is the last chapter, where Conrad tries to conclude this conflict of spiritual anxieties. The last page of the printed text of *Victory* gives as the dates when Conrad began and finished "October 1912–May 1914." The "Notes to the First Edition" are more specific about the last date. There Conrad reports: "The last of this novel was written on the 29th of May, 1914." Then Conrad calls attention to his debt to Paul: "And that last word was the single word of the title" (*Victory*, p. vii), implying that it had come to him on completing the manuscript. The dates are incorrect, however. Conrad actually began work on "Dollars," as it was then called, in April, 1912, and he had been thinking about it at least since the end of 1911.[21] The date of completion is a month off. In the left margin of the last page of the manuscript Conrad has circled the words "Capel House 27 June 1914." The difference is minor, but it may tell us that Conrad knew that he had botched his ending.

If Jessie Conrad's memory is correct, what Conrad had completed on May 29 was the penultimate chapter. In a note in her copy of *Victory*, Jessie recalls that Conrad

[21] Ibid., p. 714; Joseph Conrad, *A Conrad Memorial Library*, ed. George T. Keating, p. 252.

had been "fighting his way to the end," even taking "his meals alone for two or three weeks." On "29 May 1914," she was outside talking to the gardener when Conrad threw open an upstairs window and shouted, "'She's dead, Jess!'" The startled Jessie asked who had died, and Conrad replied, "'Why Lena, of course, and I have got the title: it is "Victory."'"[22]

So the title was not "the last word." The final chapter remained. Except for that last chapter, almost all of the manuscript is written on faint green, lined, legal-sized paper; a few pages are on 8-by-11-inch paper of the same kind. But pages 1129–39 are done on 7-by-9-inch white, unlined letter paper. Here the name Heyst appears for the first time (MS, p. 1130). The corrected manuscript is very close to the final version, and these pages may have been composed quickly, at a sitting.

Perhaps Conrad insists on the May date because he hated the actual ending. Perhaps he planned to redo it. We know that the corrected typescript that Conrad sent to John Quinn did not include the final chapter.[23] Even admirers of *Victory* dislike it.[24] Its hurried pace and perfunctory tone are at odds with the rest of the novel. Conrad was in a bind. Not only would it be strange to end with Jones, Ricardo, and Pedro still ranging Samburan, but focus must return to Heyst. The nub of the problem, however, is that the spiritual conflict must be faced down. If Conrad had ended with the penultimate chapter or if he had, in Moser's words, had Heyst "saved by his love for Lena," he would be another Paul celebrating Christian love. That would not do. Conrad was too plainly not a

---

[22] Conrad, *Conrad Memorial Library*, ed. Keating, pp. 253–54.
[23] Frederick R. Karl, *A Reader's Guide to Joseph Conrad*, p. 266.
[24] For example, ibid., p. 248.

celebrant of salvation through self-abnegation. Had he adequately rendered Lena's delusion, the issue would be less complicated. But he had not, so he was driven to the perfunctory ending that emphasizes how wrong was Lena that there would be "'no more'" death. Yet the ending is thematically confused sophistry. Heyst's pagan journey into the flames with the body of his beloved denies her fight against spiritual death, but we are treated to his final words that affirm the Christian virtues of love and hope (*Victory,* p. 410). Jones's drowning, in Conrad's over-extended symbolism, is the death of Death. Thus Lena's deed is effectual: "Death [has been] swallowed up in victory." Small wonder Conrad preferred to forget his ending.

The speciousness of Heyst's last words is especially forgettable, for he has learned nothing. Had Conrad elected to retain some strands of the manuscript and refine them—in particular Berg's metaphysical desire and Lena's erotic religiosity—he might have taken Heyst to a powerful recognition. Heyst must learn why Lena acted as she did, that she was unaware of her motive and that he shares her delusion. There are technical problems with such a recognition, to be sure, but that ending seems implicit in the manuscript. As it is, Heyst dies ignorant, despite Conrad's attempt to make us think otherwise. One can invoke irony, of course, arguing that we are supposed to see that Heyst's last words testify to his ignorance. The argument would rescue a part of the ending. But a part only. And I detect no signs of dramatic irony in Heyst's farewell.

Wish as he might, Conrad could not end with the penultimate chapter, and the ending he gives merely exemplifies his inability to render the religious dementia he had wanted to write of. To depict holy madness had been one of his conscious intentions. But his deeper impulse may have told him that he did not know whereof he spoke.

Conrad's desire to write about deviant religious experience goes back to the 1890s and the uncompleted novel *The Sisters*.[25] The first of its two parts treats a Russian exile and painter, Stephen, who searches for God in the "unveiled religion of art." Yet Stephen doubts the sanctity of his quest. His "aspirations . . . presented themselves to him sometimes as a plot of the powers of darkness for the destruction of his soul." Yet wherever Stephen goes to find the visible hand of God, "the hand of man seemed to raise an unscalable wall between him and his Maker." He considers going to deserts but fears "their deception. They would also speak in glorious promises only to cast him down at last from the pinnacle of his expectations." This reference to Jesus' temptation in the wilderness (Matt. 4:1-11) suggests that Stephen fears the demands of the mystic union as much as he craves its satisfactions and thus courts deception and failure in his quest. It is an attractive character sketch of a person who desires and fears religious experience, but Garnett urged Conrad to give up *The Sisters,* and he did, at least in its original form. The second part, dealing with the sisters, Teresa and Rita, found its way into *The Arrow of Gold,* while strands of the Stephen section were worked into various later novels. Kurtz, too, is a painter whose quest leads him over the edge of a precipice. The theme of Christian conflict enters into *Nostromo,* and, as Stanley Tick has argued pursuing a thesis close to my own, there the theme leads

[25] Joseph Conrad, *The Sisters*, published in 1928.

141

to unintended ambiguities.[26] Razumov is another Russian exile trapped between opposing ideologies that have in common religious fanaticism. And Axel Heyst is another wanderer from the north, and in the manuscript also a painter,[27] caught up in a drama of religious delusions. Conrad, then, did not quite do Garnett's bidding, for, despite his many avowals of agnosticism, the problem of religious experience seems to have intrigued him too much to let Stephen of *The Sisters* die.

Why? Possibly he thought there would be money in it. In a letter of May 18, 1907, to Pinker, Conrad says, ". . . my mind runs much on popularity now. . . . Apart from religious problems the public mind runs on questions of war and peace and labour. . . . In short, my idea is to treat those subjects in a novel with a sufficiently interesting story, whose notion has come into my head lately."[28] Conrad's phrasing seems to mean that "religious problems" are obviously the hottest item with the public, and Conrad's dalliance with such problems from *The Sisters* to *Victory* might have been inspired by his relative poverty. The sales of *Victory* proved him correct, perhaps. The "novel with a sufficiently interesting story," however, may have come into Conrad's head as he was writing Pinker, whose anxieties Conrad often sought to allay by fictions of fictions. But if Conrad means what he says, we may have in this letter the first reference to what was to become *Victory*. If so, from the outset Conrad may have

---

[26]Stanley Tick, "The Gods of *Nostromo*," *MFS* 10 (Spring, 1964):15–26.

[27]Berg's New Guinea wanderings were a quest for subjects for his art: "They were water colors and in them the fierce tropical nature and the physiognomies of cannibals appeared as if seen through a softening mist" (MS, p. 19).

[28]Jean-Aubry, *Joseph Conrad*, 2:49.

seen its "religious problems" as so many pound notes. Until that afternoon in May, 1914, *Victory* was titled "Because of the Dollars."

Yet I doubt Conrad was that cynical. Poverty alone would not have inspired two and a half years of that kind of very hard work, and Conrad's financial worries had eased by the time he began *Victory*. Another source of Conrad's desire to write a novel of religious experience would be his Polish heritage. The poetic dramas of the Polish romantics, in particular those of Adam Mickiewicz and Zygmunt Krasiński, ordinarily place their protagonists in spiritual crisis to the end of affirming Christian values, which is to say that they were intensely patriotic.[29] Such themes, then, were very familiar to Conrad, and treating them himself he might have seen as a link with his past. Indeed, it was while Conrad was working on *Victory* that he planned to return to Poland, a trip that took place as soon as all work on the novel was over. So Conrad's Polish background may be behind the vagaries of *Victory*.

A more negative inspiration might have worked upon Conrad, too. Coincident with the writing of *Victory* are Conrad's virulent attacks on Dostoevski, Tolstoy, and their Christianity. In a letter to Garnett dated May 27, 1912, Conrad reviles Dostoevski's "fierce mouthings from some prehistoric ages," and two years later, on February 23, 1914, when he was winding up *Victory*, Conrad writes again to Garnett that he objects to "the base from which Tolstoy starts—Christianity," which "has lent itself with amazing facility to cruel distortion."[30] Coming when it

[29]Thus Conrad once reminded his aunt that "with us religion and patriotism are closely akin." Conrad, *Letters to Poradowska*, ed. and trans. Gee and Sturm, p. 78, letter of September 8, 1894.

[30]Joseph Conrad, *Letters*, ed. Edward Garnett, pp. 240–41, 245.

does, this criticism surely has a bearing on *Victory*, a work meant to illustrate those cruel distortions of Christianity. The intended theme of *Victory* invades Russian territory, and the novel may have been meant to sustain Conrad's attacks on Dostoevski's mouthings and Tolstoy's base.

Whatever the motives prompting Conrad to attempt the theme of religious experience, he is in alien territory, perhaps frightened by it, too. He cannot grasp the personalities of individuals in a religious crisis, the scriptural reinforcements are too weak, and in his problematic ending Conrad overextends the line of his symbolism. But it is a fascinating defeat.

CONCLUSION

Unlikely as it may seem to jaded readers, I have been conservative. Allusions incidental or of slight metaphorical value have been passed over, and I have kept in the main to specific verbal allusions where the context makes it reasonably certain that Conrad has the Bible in mind. Two things remain to do—one a matter of fact, the other of speculation. The matter of fact is to demonstrate that Conrad uses the King James version rather than the other likely candidate, the Douay-Rheims. The speculative problem is why Conrad turns in the later phase of his career to parody.

Except for one problematic instance, where discrepancies exist between the King James and Douay renditions of a Conradian allusion, King James is incontestably the source. The exception appears in "The End of the Tether," and a dubious one because a question of spelling. For the storeroom where Massey finds the iron pieces that wreck the *Sofala* the narrator fashions a curious metaphor: "A complete and impervious blackness pervaded that Capharnaum of forgotten things" (p. 323). This is the Douay spelling of the town in which Jesus begins his ministry and which he

145

later curses for rejecting him: "And thou Capharnaum, shalt thou be exalted up to heaven? thou shalt go down even unto hell" (Matt. 11:23). In the three editions I have consulted, the King James scholars spell the name of the town worse than Sodom "Capernaum." This is the only instance known to me where Conrad might be using the Douay version. Perhaps Massey is Catholic. But the addition of a consonant should not persuade a jury.

That peculiar case aside, where discrepancies, and more substantial ones than that, exist, King James is the choice. For example, the allusions to the tale of Cain in "The Secret Sharer" come from the Authorized Version. It would be passing strange did they not, since Leggatt is another of Conrad's sons from a parsonage. Leggatt quotes for us: "'What does the Bible say? "Driven off the face of the earth." Very well. I am off the face of the earth now'" (p. 132). Leggatt remembers the Authorized verb, for which Douay gives "cast . . . out" (Gen. 4:14). More persuasive is the passage from "Youth" out of Job, describing the fired *Judea:* "And from the cone of flame the sparks flew upwards, as man is born to trouble, to leaky ships, and to ships that burn" (p. 31). Douay reads, "Man is born to labour and the birds to fly"; King James, "Yet man is born unto trouble, as the sparks fly upward" (Job 5:7). No doubt there. Another Job allusion, Jones's "'coming and going up and down the earth'" (*Victory*, pp. 317–18) is also far closer to King James's than to Douay's Satan, who says, "I have gone round about the earth, and walked through it" (1:7, 2:2). In *Victory* again, when we are told that Heyst "didn't toil or spin visibly" (p. 16), Conrad refers to the Authorized lilies of the field; Douay's do not "labour." Similarly, when Conrad mentions the "outer darkness" that besets that compelled guest to the wedding feast (Matt. 22:13) just before Lingard comes to Edith Travers "'like a thief in the night'" (p. 153), he is remembering King James; Douay reads "exterior darkness" (see also *Rescue,* p. 385; "Karain," p. 73). A final specimen comes from *A Personal Record,* a gratuitous allusion to John 3:8. Conrad jibes at this modern world "where the journalists read the signs of the sky, and the wind of heaven itself, blowing where it listeth, does so under the prophetical management of the Meteorological Office" (p. 91). Against Douay's ethereal rendering, "The Spirit breatheth where he will; and thou hearest his voice," the Authorized Version prefers Conrad's translation: "The wind bloweth where it listeth, and thou hearest the sound thereof."

The evidence, then, is persuasive for the Authorized Version. Circumstance favors it too, of course. King James is the Bible of English literary tradition, and Conrad probably had to cope with it on his way to becoming a master mariner in the British Merchant Service, even if, like Captain Allistoun in *The Nigger of the "Narcissus,"* he passed on the chore of reading it at burials to his first mate (the fifteenth chapter of 1 Corinthians was obligatory, following the "De profundis"). Whatever version the gentleman of Ratcliffe highway thrust upon Conrad, he found King James at sea, and it played its part in attuning Conrad's ear to English prose.

According to Jessie Conrad, the burial service was on Conrad's delirious lips as he lay almost dying in the first two months of 1910.[1] Like many another critic before me, I suspect that Conrad's breakdown after finishing the first draft of *Under Western Eyes* may not be unrelated to the changes in his art, in particular to the change from Scripture as normative guide to Scripture parodied.

---

[1] Jessie Conrad, *Joseph Conrad and His Circle,* p. 144.

But I should rehearse the main lines of this study. First, I have not made rigid distinctions. Parody appears in early Conrad, for example, in "Youth." On the whole, though, Scripture's normative status intensifies through *The Secret Agent.* As I have remarked, were we to disregard what is not in *The Secret Agent*—any glimmer of a positive vision of God and man in history—the novel could be mistaken for Christian art, a midrash on Jesus' sermon. An extravagant way of putting it, but almost just. If I am correct, however, the change to relentless parody is detectable in Conrad's next novel, *Under Western Eyes.* The change, then, is sudden, and it becomes severe. After *Under Western Eyes* parody of Scripture so dominates that one who does not perceive its workings cannot appreciate *Chance, Victory,* and *The Rescue.* Finally, my notion of "decline" may offend opponents of rhetorical dualism, but it has the virtue of matching Conrad's perdurably dualistic mind. I have argued that *Chance, Victory,* and *The Rescue* are thoroughly parodic works remarkable for their pervasive and genial contempt. They are morally tainted. Yet by standard aesthetic criteria, such as ambition, originality, complex interweaving of image and idea, and intricate epistemologies, all three works approach brilliance. Conrad's artistic powers do not "decline" after the breakdown; in some respects they increase. The decline is in Conrad's moral, not in his artistic, powers. One classic view of later Conrad could not be more mistaken, that later Conrad reveals his imaginative failure in depicting a "new cleansed moral universe."[2] The "moral universe" of later Conrad is a black hole. Are we supposed to laugh at Lord Jim, at Emilia Gould, at Winnie Verloc? I doubt it. But we are supposed to laugh aloud at Marlow,

2 Albert Guerard, *Conrad the Novelist,* p. 257.

at Lena, at King Tom Lingard, and at everything human in the inverted worlds of *Chance, Victory,* and *The Rescue.* They are brilliantly polished mirrors reflecting their maker's moral contortions, his baffled rage.

If Conrad was murmuring the fifteenth chapter of 1 Corinthians in January and February, 1910, that could suggest that some species of religious feeling played a part in Conrad's breakdown. As Karl says of the affair, Conrad "was Yanko Gooral again."[3] Bernard Meyer, fully competent to pass judgment upon the causes and nature of Conrad's illness, calls it a "psychotic delirium" probably brought about by the journey into his Polish years that *Under Western Eyes* required.[4] Those "mystic vaticinations" that the professor detests may, then, memorialize the mysticism of Apollo Korzeniowski, which Conrad perhaps remembered with love and loathing. Not unlike Stephen of *The Sisters,* Conrad may have been attracted to and repelled by the idea of intense personal religious experience, of ending like the father he describes in a letter (January 20, 1900) to Edward Garnett: "A man of great sensibilities; of exalted and dreamy temperament; with a terrible gift of irony and of gloomy disposition; withal, of strong religious feeling, degenerating after the loss of his wife into mysticism touched with despair."[5] Recovering from his illness, Conrad writes (May 17, 1910) to John Galsworthy, "Anything better than black depression, which may be the sign of religious mania."[6] Slight evidence, hardly better than an added consonant, but it suggests that Conrad himself detected in his "psychotic delir-

---

[3]Frederick R. Karl, *Joseph Conrad: The Three Lives,* p. 681.
[4]Bernard C. Meyer, *Joseph Conrad: A Psychoanalytic Biography,* pp. 210–11.
[5]G. Jean-Aubry, *Joseph Conrad: Life and Letters,* 1:292.
[6]Ibid., 2:108.

ium" some frightening form of "strong religious feeling."

I have said that Conrad may have had trouble depicting strong religious feeling in *Victory* because it was not a part of him. It is also possible that it was too much a part. Perhaps he, too, makes the great refusal out of fear. The torrent of scriptural allusions that pours out of the later work could betoken fright as readily as contempt.

All this is speculative, of course. We know neither Conrad's fall nor his wrestling. We can only read the signs on the wall of his fiction, and never with the prophet's certainty. This much is reasonably certain: that in the English Bible Conrad found a way to enter the traditions of English literature; that he often found in Scripture metaphors equal to his feelings about art and reality; that the Bible furnished images of history against which Conrad could fashion his own image of radical discontinuity. Without the English Bible, Conrad would not have been the writer we know.

BIBLIOGRAPHY

Amiel, Henri-Frédéric. *Fragments d'un journal intime.* 10th ed. 2 vols. Genève: Georg & Co., 1908.

Baines, Jocelyn. *Joseph Conrad: A Critical Biography.* New York: McGraw-Hill, 1967.

Bonney, William W. *Thorns & Arabesques: Contexts for Conrad's Fiction.* Baltimore, Md., and London: Johns Hopkins University Press, 1980.

Bradbrook, Muriel C. *Joseph Conrad: Poland's English Genius.* 1941. Reprint. New York: Russell and Russell, 1965.

Conrad, Jessie. *Joseph Conrad and His Circle.* New York: Dutton, 1935.

Conrad, Joseph. *Collected Edition of the Works of Joseph Conrad.* London: J. M. Dent, 1946–55.

———. *Conrad to a Friend: 150 Selected Letters from Joseph Conrad to Richard Curle.* Edited by Richard Curle. Garden City, N.Y.: Doubleday, Doran, 1928.

———. *Joseph Conrad's Letters to R. B. Cunninghame Graham.* Edited by C. T. Watts. London: Cambridge University Press, 1969.

———. *Letters from Joseph Conrad, 1895–1924.* Edited by Edward Garnett. Indianapolis: Bobbs-Merrill, 1928.

———. *Letters of Joseph Conrad to Marguerite Poradowska, 1880–1920.* Edited and translated by John A. Gee and Paul J. Sturm. New Haven, Conn.: Yale University Press, 1940.

———. *Lord Jim.* Edited by Thomas C. Moser. New York: W. W. Norton, 1968.

———. *The Sisters.* New York: Crosby, Gaige, 1928.

Dike, Donald A. "The Tempest of Axel Heyst." *Nineteenth-Century Fiction* 17 (September, 1962):95–113.

Dowden, Wilfred P. *Joseph Conrad: The Imaged Style.* Nashville, Tenn.: Vanderbilt University Press, 1970.

Flamm, Dudley. "The Ambiguous Nazarene in *Lord Jim.*" *English Literature in Transition* 9 (1968):35–37.

Fleishman, Avrom. *Conrad's Politics.* Baltimore, Md.: Johns Hopkins University Press, 1967.

Ford, Ford Madox. "Decennial." *London Mercury* 32 (July, 1935): 223–31.

———. *Joseph Conrad: A Personal Remembrance.* 1924. Reprint. New York: Octagon Books, 1965.

Forster, E. M. *A Passage to India.* New York: Harcourt, Brace, 1924.

Frye, Northrop. *Anatomy of Criticism: Four Essays.* 1957. Reprint. New York: Atheneum, 1966.

Fussell, Paul. *The Great War and Modern Memory.* New York and London: Oxford University Press, 1975.

Gillon, Adam. "The Merchant of Esmeralda: Conrad's Archetypal Jew." *Polish Review* 9 (Autumn, 1964):3–20.

Goldknopf, David. *The Life of the Novel.* Chicago and London: University of Chicago Press, 1972.

Gose, Elliott B. "Pure Exercise of Imagination: Archetypal Symbolism in *Lord Jim.*" *PMLA* 79 (March, 1964):137–47.

Graver, Lawrence. *Conrad's Short Fiction.* Berkeley and Los Angeles: University of California Press, 1969.

Gross, Seymour L. "The Devil in Samburan: Jones and Ricardo in *Victory.*" *Nineteenth-Century Fiction* 16 (June, 1961):81–85.

Guerard, Albert. *Conrad the Novelist.* 1958. Reprint. New York: Atheneum, 1967.

Guetti, James. *The Limits of Metaphor.* Ithaca, N.Y.: Cornell University Press, 1967.

Hay, Eloise Knapp. *The Political Novels of Joseph Conrad.* Chicago and London: University of Chicago Press, 1963.

Henn, T. R. *The Lonely Tower.* London: Methuen, 1965.

Hoene-Wronski, Josef Marie. *Philosophie absolue de l'histoire.* 2 vols. Paris: Amyot, 1852.

Jean-Aubry, G. *Joseph Conrad: Life and Letters.* 2 vols. Garden City, N.Y.: Doubleday, Page, 1927.

Jeffares, Norman. *A Commentary on the Collected Poems of W. B. Yeats.* Stanford, Calif.: Stanford University Press, 1968.

Kahele, Sharon, and Howard German. "Conrad's *Victory:* A Reassessment." *Modern Fiction Studies* 10 (Spring, 1964):55–72.

Karl, Frederick R. *Joseph Conrad: The Three Lives.* New York: Farrar, Straus, Giroux, 1979.

———. *A Reader's Guide to Joseph Conrad.* New York: Noonday Press, 1960.

Keating, George T., ed. *A Conrad Memorial Library.* Garden City, N.Y.: Doubleday, Doran, 1929.

Kohn, Hans. *Pan-Slavism: Its History and Ideology.* 2d ed., rev. New York: Vintage Books, 1960.

Leiter, Louis H. "Echo Structures: Conrad's 'The Secret Sharer.'" *Twentieth Century Literature* 5 (January, 1960):159–75.

Levin, Gerald H. "An Allusion to Tasso in Conrad's *Chance.*" *Nineteenth-Century Fiction* 13 (September, 1958):145–51.

Lewis, R. W. B. *Trials of the Word.* New Haven, Conn., and London: Yale University Press, 1965.

Mathews, James W. "Ironic Symbolism in Conrad's 'Youth.'" *Studies in Short Fiction* 11 (1974):117–23.

Meyer, Bernard. *Joseph Conrad: A Psychoanalytic Biography.* Princeton, N.J.: Princeton University Press, 1967.

Miller, J. Hillis. *Poets of Reality.* New York: Atheneum, 1969.

Miłosz, Czesław. "Apollo Korzeniowski: Joseph Conrad's Father." *Mosaic* 6 (1972):121–40.

———. *The History of Polish Literature.* London: Macmillan, 1969.

Morf, Gustav. *The Polish Shades and Ghosts of Joseph Conrad.* New York: Astra Books, 1976.

Moser, Thomas P. *Joseph Conrad: Achievement and Decline.* 1957. Reprint. Hamden, Conn.: Arebon Books, 1966.

Palmer, John A. *Joseph Conrad's Fiction: A Study in Literary Growth.* Ithaca, N.Y.: Cornell University Press, 1968.

Park, Douglas B. "Conrad's *Victory:* The Anatomy of a Pose." *Nineteenth-Century Fiction* 31 (1976):150–69.

Raphael, Alice. *Goethe the Challenger.* New York: Jonathan Cape, 1932.

Rosenfield, Claire. *Paradise of Snakes: An Archetypal Analysis of Conrad's Political Novels.* Chicago: University of Chicago Press, 1967.

Schwarz, Daniel R. *Conrad: "Almayer's Folly" to "Under Western Eyes."* Ithaca, N.Y.: Cornell University Press, 1980.

———. "The Journey to Patusan: The Educations of Jim and Marlow in Conrad's *Lord Jim.*" *Studies in the Novel* 4 (Fall, 1972):442–58.

Tick, Stanley. "The Gods of *Nostromo.*" *Modern Fiction Studies* 10 (Spring, 1964):15–26.

Tillyard, E. M. W. *The Epic Strain in the English Novel.* London: Chatto & Windus, 1963.

Watt, Ian. "*Almayer's Folly:* Memories and Models." *Mosaic* 8 (Fall, 1974):165–82.

———. *Conrad in the Nineteenth Century.* Berkeley and Los Angeles: University of California Press, 1979.

———. "Conrad's Preface to *The Nigger of the 'Narcissus.'*" *Novel* 7 (Winter, 1974):101-15.

Watts, C. T. *Conrad's "Heart of Darkness": A Critical and Contextual Discussion.* Milan: Mursia International, 1977.

Widmer, Kingsley. "Conrad's Pyrrhic *Victory.*" *Twentieth-Century Literature* 5 (October, 1959):123–30.

Ziolkowski, Theodore. *Fictional Transfigurations of Jesus.* Princeton, N.J.: Princeton University Press, 1972.

INDEX

Designed by Bill Cason, *Joseph Conrad's Bible* was composed by the University of Oklahoma Press in various sizes of Olympus (Trump Mediaeval), with calligraphic display on the title page. The printing was done by Thomson-Shore, with binding by John H. Dekker & Sons. The paper used for this volume is 60# Glatfelter.